Change Points

Books by Joyce Landorf

Let's Have a Banquet
Joyce, I Feel Like I Know You
His Stubborn Love
To Lib or Not to Lib
The Richest Lady in Town
Mourning Song
Mix Butter With Love
For These Fragile Times
The Fragrance of Beauty
Tough and Tender
I Came to Love You Late
Joseph
Changepoints: When We Need Him Most

Change points

When we need Him most

Joyce Landorf

Fleming H. Revell Company
Old Tappan, New Jersey

Library of Congress Cataloging in Publication Data

Landorf, Joyce.
Changepoints, when we need Him most.

Includes bibliographical references.
1. Women–Conduct of life. 2. Women–Religious life.
3. Landorf, Joyce. I. Title.
BJ1610.L27   248.8'43   81–11900
ISBN 0–8007–1257–9   AACR2

As usual
praise and blessings
upon the heads of
Brenda Arnold, Sheila Rapp and
all the editors at Revell
for all their untiring efforts!

Contents

1
Changepoints...
When You Need Him Most

This time, like all times, is a very good one if we but know what to do with it.

RALPH WALDO EMERSON

The Bible-study class was over. More than a hundred enthusiastic women from all over the California desert and various parts of the United States and Canada had more than filled Betty Manning's luxurious home.

I was teaching a series of lessons based on my book *The High Cost of Growing*, and the atmosphere had fairly crackled with the sounds of stretching minds and the unseen but real presence of the Lord. A contagious type of joy passed about the room, and I thought to myself, *No teacher has ever been taught more by her students than I.*

After the closing prayer I was surrounded by a noisy hubbub of questions, comments, quick hellos and goodbyes, and gentle hugs. It was a special time for me; yet, in spite of the press of women around me, and out of the corner of my eye, I saw her.

She was standing apart from the others, just quietly

waiting, the last in line. She was young, quite beautiful, and obviously quite upset.

When the last person said good-bye, the young woman came up, hugged me, and tearfully whispered, "Oh, Joyce, thank you for today's lesson. I really needed it." Then, taking a deep breath for the sake of some semblance of control, she added, "Do pray for me . . . I'm at the changepoints of my life."

Long after, I promised her I'd pray, and all the way home. I kept thinking about her word *changepoints*.

My big forty-pound dictionary does not list the one compound word—only the two words, *change* and *points*. Still, the woman had put them together, and I knew exactly what she'd meant.

"Changepoints of my life," she had said. Funny, but isn't that exactly where we all are most of the time? Aren't all people in the midst of transition?

Look at some of the definitions of the word *change* when it's used as a verb: "to cause to turn, to pass from one state to another, to alter, to make a difference, to vary, or to substitute one thing for another." Then, as a noun, *change* can mean, "any variation or alteration in form, state, quality or essence, or the beginning." The word *point* has over thirty-five definitions, most of which pertain to or describe a position, place, fixed station, particular time, a unit of measurement, the end of something, or a main idea.

As I studied the long, detailed definitions of both words, I realized that the young woman in my class had created a new word for a very old situation.

The circumstances of our lives put us in constant contact with points of change, and just when we feel we are freed from one particular changepoint, crisis, transition, or stage of life—pow! We are off into another one. Changepoints are here to stay.

The little girl can't wait to grow up so she can be a "boss" like Mommy.

The teenage girl fantasizes about having clear, beautiful skin and what kind of a man she'll love.

The young wife and new mother longs for the time when her baby will sleep the whole night through.

The wife of a military man dreams of OWNING a home, wallpapering it, and staying in it until the cow jumps over the moon.

The couple without children wonders if having or adopting a child would bring a lasting happiness to their marriage.

The mother of two teenagers hopes the old adage "this too shall pass" will come true.

The woman whose children have grown and left home can't define exactly what's wrong with her—only that this time in her life isn't as she expected it to be.

The newly divorced or widowed woman suddenly finds herself experiencing the highly praised freedom she's heard about, but now that she has it, it's a lonely kind of freedom and she doesn't have a clue as to how to develop or use it.

The woman who goes through the hormonal changes of menopause wakes up one morning to find the cold fear of growing old heavily upon her. She questions whether God has more in store for her or if this is all there is.

What we all forget in every phase of our lives is that *life* is a whole *series* of changepoints.

Did my young student think that as I grew older, I matured and left my changepoints behind me? Or, did she mistakenly conclude that since I was *teaching*, I must have it all together, and therefore I'm not threatened or intimidated by changepoints?

I smiled when I got to thinking about people who *appear* to have it all together, because no one—not even the incredible Billy Graham or *Mrs.* Billy Graham—has it all together twenty-four hours a day, every day.

At this very moment we are all facing the changepoints of our lives, and if we are honest we'll have to admit that at times it's rather frightening! Only some of our circumstances like age, environment, and the state of our physical, emotional, and spiritual well-being, will be different. But none of us can avoid the pressures and stress of change for very long.

Even my four-year-old granddaughter, April Joy, is at a changepoint in her little life. Granted, hers involves not getting to go to her beloved preschool this summer, and mine involves a book deadline, but for both of us these changepoints have invaded, reshaped, and rearranged our lives. We never seem to outgrow the movements of life, and with each movement comes change that often baffles, irritates, and even frightens us.

It appears that our panic and resentment toward changepoints in our lives begins in the genesis of our existence. Early on we develop a concept about what we *think* life, our life, will be all about: what kind of person we'll be, what we'll do, who we'll marry, or how rich and famous we'll be.

Rarely is it an accurate picture. The problem stems from the fact that each of us tends to fantasize. We see our lives from an *ideal* point of view rather than from the *real* —where they actually are.

As we grow up, the *ideal* concept and the unvarnished *real* begin to clash, and when we begin to measure or compare the two, we are dismayed to find the *real* always wins. The ideal concept begins to break apart, and sometimes this happens even in childhood.

These ideals we have set for ourselves are often placed too far above our abilities and strengths, so that when we fall short of the high expectations, we are sadly disillusioned.

We want—no, we demand—and expect entirely too much from every stage of life, from every experience, and most of all, from every relationship. We don't think too much about change. We simply anticipate staying in control and gradually becoming totally comfortable.

There is hardly any room in our perfect little world for changepoints, so when they come—and they do come with nauseating regularity—we panic or are at least offended.

Granted, some changepoints are very small. I remember that when I fell and cut or bruised my knees as a child, my mother washed my wound and gave me lots of TLC, but she also mentioned that nobody at the White House in Washington would think a whole lot about my misfortune. It was good training because I learned how to handle the nitty-gritty changepoints like missing a bus, tripping over one's own feet, failing a test, or getting a traffic ticket, quite well. Most of us have learned to adjust our attitudes and responses to these bothersome changes. But we are not about to accept changepoints as calmly when we are fired from a job, sued for divorce or malpractice, faced with filing bankruptcy, or when we are unable to recover from surgery, an accident, or the loss of a loved one. Suddenly, what we pictured our lives as being is no where *near* reality. It appears that *some* incidental changes, hindrances, variations, or substitutes are acceptable, even tolerable; but the abrupt, about-face, this-could-never-have-happened changes are shocking, and they give our souls a good shaking.

My friend Dr. Charles Swindoll suggests in his book on marriage, *Strike the Original Match,* that the term *honeymoon* be changed to the *adjustment period.* He calls *adjustment* the best and proper description for those early days of marriage. Even if the term is unromantic and "sounds like a quick trip to the chiropractor's office," his suggestion is most astute. I've been married twenty-eight years now, and there are times when I think both Dick and I are still in the "adjustment period" of our lives.

I guess I'd go a step further and say that most of life, because of the changepoints, represents an ongoing adjustment period.

Consider this for a moment. About the time I got over the hideous junior-high phase of life and was finally adjusting to the roller coaster emotions of a teenager, I turned twenty and got married. Then, before I discovered any ancient or new clues about marriage, I was up to my earlobes in babies, formula, and dirty diapers. Every time I turned around, I was dealing with yet another changepoint.

If you have read my book *His Stubborn Love,* you know that in the midst of all this, in our fifth year of marriage, the miracle of all miracles took place. Both Dick and I had the unforgettable experience of becoming truly born again on the very same day, in different places, without either of us knowing what God was doing for the other.

Almost immediately I thought, *Aha! Now that we have Christ in our lives, nothing is going to rock our boat or sink it. Not change, frustration, failure, or disappointments—nothing, absolutely nothing.*

I reasoned that given some growing time in the Lord—to raise our children, to make Dick's job and finances a little more secure, and after finally getting to a place where I wouldn't have to cook hamburger 150 different ways—*then* we'd really have it all together. I sincerely believed that by attaining a certain degree of physical, emotional, and spiritual maturity, I'd never have a problem with the frustrations of changepoints. Or, at the very least, I'd be able to accept change and its inevitable confusion with the same effortless grace I'd be able to serve Roast Duck à l'Orange plus all the trimmings, ending with Rum Chocolate Mousse, for twenty-four people at a sitdown dinner.

In other words, someday I'd have it together! However, the facts of life prove that this oversimplification about maturing into some kind of a projected ideal that we have carefully cherished is quite a fragile thing. It's easily smashed and fragmented.

The demolition of our ideals may happen early in our life, through relationships with our parents or through school experiences—and later, through death, divorce, the "empty nest syndrome," or even retirement. But happen it will! And when it does, we never seem to be prepared for the shocking confrontation with change.

Sometimes, because we are Christians and don't want anyone to doubt our spirituality or question our theological depth, we give the impression to others that changepoints are to be treated as one treats a darling little puppy. Ignore his mess on the new carpet and the fact that he is systematically shredding our favorite couch to ribbons. After all, he's cute, cuddly, and easy to forgive. In short, we suffer from tunnel vision and so we think, *Oh, he'll grow up, and someday Fido will be a dignified dog.* We leave a lot to time and maturity. In reality, discipline, education, and lots of practice make a puddle-making puppy into a "Joe Cool" Snoopy dog.

To blunder through our Christian life, ignoring the presence of change, is to ignore the inevitable and to be put into a state of panic each time we stand at a changepoint of our lives.

Change, like an octopus, rises out of the sea, stares at us with cold, naked reality, and wraps its tentacles of fear, loneliness, pain, and frustration tightly around us!

When my young friend in my Bible study asked me to pray for her, she did so because she had taken all the blinders off her eyes. Probably for the first time she was facing an incredible reality, that even though she was a dedicated child of God, the octopus of change was scaring her silly! How I loved her honesty.

The Apostle Paul wrote to the Philippians, ". . . I have learned, in whatever state I am, to be content" (Philippians 4:11 RSV). I wish he'd expanded just a bit on that one word, *learned*, because I have a feeling that if he had denied the changepoints in his life, or implied that change did not bother him, he would never have had to *learn* how to be content. He simply would have written, "I am content." Instead, he wrote, "I *have learned,*" and his use of the past tense suggests that it took some time and was not an overnight realization!

The changepoints in the lives of Adam, Noah, Abraham, Sarah, Isaac, Rebekah, Jacob, Rachel, Joseph, Moses, and David (the list is endless) gave each of them times of great tension and the inevitable feeling of being abandoned by God.

The thrilling thing to see, however, was that no matter how change gripped their lives and threatened to paralyze, the sovereignty of God and His great plan was always accomplished. There must have been countless times when those great men and women of God resented the changepoints in their lives, didn't understand them; yet, somehow and by some special God-given grace, they *learned* to accept change. Consequently, God's beautiful purpose was carried out by mere frightened mortals, in spite of their fearsome apprehensions.

I'm glad the writers of the Scriptures left those giants of faith with their fears, loneliness, and frustrations plainly visible. It helps me to know, in a *real* way, that my perfect little world, the one I want to see so badly, is rarely going to be perfect. In fact, no number of spiritual rationalizations or tired clichés can make it so.

Lest you think I should be more positive, more upbeat, and that I should quit painting such a dark picture, let me quickly answer you that I *do* have brief moments of glorious perfection. Yes, that's what I said, *perfection*. There are times when I *know* I've done very well, or God allows a relationship to be healed, and the victory leaves me heady with joy. At these times, I experience a marvelous wholeness in Christ. But, at the same time, I must not be blind about the way sin and Satan have crippled our world and our thinking. For life in the real world has a way of shattering the desired perfection we long to possess on a regular basis.

The point of this book is not to inform you that in this life you'll be squeezed beyond belief by the octopus of change. That's already an established fact of life. No, I hope here to explain some of our responses to change, to perhaps learn about coping with change, and lastly, to check out the real "needs" versus the "wants" of our lives.

I'm writing this to me as well. For often, when in those rare moments I'm walking tall, thinking I've learned a few valuable lessons lately, "Pow!" reality's fist hits me in the solar plexus of my life, and I moan, "Oh, no! Not a changepoint again?"

God's answer is gentle but direct, "Yes, Joyce—again."

A few weeks ago, when a new stage and a change in my life's direction came abruptly into view, I did what I have done many times before. First, I panicked. Then, I cried. Finally, as the tears flushed some of the cobwebs out of my mind, the Lord urged me to do what I've done a thousand times before. I sat down at the piano and began leafing through my hymnal.

On page 329 of Lexicon's *The New Church Hymnal,*
the song I was looking for beamed warmly up at me like
an old friend. Funny. Although it was written in 1908, it's
still a song for now—a moment-by-moment song. A song
that reaches deeply into all my living levels—and will into
yours if you give it a chance.

Slowly and out of its bouncy rhythm, I began to sing the
words.

> Just when I need Him
> Jesus is near,
> Just when I falter,
> Just when I fear;
> Ready to help me,
> Ready to cheer,
> Just when I need Him most.
>
> Just when I need Him most,
> Just when I need Him most;
> Jesus is near to comfort and cheer,
> Just when I need Him most.

The lyrics and melody brought the quiet confirmation
forcefully into my mind. I am not alone. The song told me
that this reluctance to accept change and the revelation
that my little world will never be quite as perfect as I'd
like it to be, is as well-known to the Father as it is to me.

When I finished all the verses of the song, it seemed that
Jesus Himself, invisible to the eye but clearly seen by my
heart, joined me on the piano bench.

In His hands was a small, gift-wrapped package.

"For me?" I asked, nodding toward His hands.

He smiled, and when the last note of the song died
away, He handed me the box.

I opened it eagerly. The present was so beautifully wrapped, I could hardly wait to see inside. But clearly the contents were disappointing.

"Lord," I questioned, "I see you've given me another changepoint. I've had so many this past year. What will I do with another one?"

He didn't speak, but I read the answer in His eyes. "When will you understand, Joyce? *This* is my *gift* to you."

Then I knew that the question was not what I'll do with another changepoint, but what *He* will do.

What had I just been singing? When do I need Him most? Ah, the gentle conviction became stronger, and I began to understand that *there is not one certain time of life, not one particular phase of growth during which we need God more than any other. All of life—each stage and each moment—is in fact, a never-ending time of needing the Lord.*

I squirmed with the pressure of those conclusions, because I always find it second nature to *resist* change. Now I've been asked to embrace it; take it as a loving gift, and gratefully, even joyfully, *run* with it.

So I must. Actually, the godless alternatives to living in today's world are totally unacceptable once you've met the Master.

Bob Hawkins, friend and publisher, reminded me the other day of Jim Elliot, the martyred missionary to Ecuador, who was once asked if he really liked wrestling. He replied:

> Before the match I'm *terrified*,
> During the match I'm in *agony*,
> And after the match I'm *exhausted*.
> But, yes, I *love* wrestling.

There it is! Our response to change must be realistic and
ever mindful of what and who can meet our needs.

Jim Elliot's words bring to mind those of Paul when he
wrote:

> We are pressed on every side by troubles,
>   but not crushed and broken.
> We are perplexed because we don't know why
>   things happen as they do, but we don't
>   give up and quit.
> We are hunted down,
>   but God never abandons us.
> We get knocked down,
>   but we get up again and keep going.
> . . . Though our bodies are dying, our inner
>   strength in the Lord is growing every day.
> These troubles and sufferings of ours
>   are, after all, quite small and won't
>   last very long.
> Yet this short time of distress will result
>   in God's richest blessing upon us
>   forever and ever!
> 2 Corinthians 4:8–10, 16, 17 TLB

Evidently Paul loved wrestling too! But we need Jesus
—before, during, and after this wrestling match called
life!

Let's look at the Father's gift of change for what it really
is—a God-devised way to heighten, deepen, and enhance
our obtainable potentials while we are in the midst of our
changepoints.

And when are we in the changepoints of our lives?
Always!

2
Changepoints...
When the Babies Come

Little Cradles

All over the earth they are swaying,
The nests where the little ones lie,
And the faces—black, brown, white or yellow,
Are watched by the Father's kind eye.

AUTHOR UNKNOWN

Perhaps you are pregnant with your first baby. Or maybe you are pregnant and already have one child. Or, worse yet, you are pregnant and already have two babies under four years of age, and the stress of it all is beginning to eat you alive. You are quite ready to shout, "Stop, world, I want to get off!"

Many times when I'm at a speaking engagement now, I look out into an audience of women, and I can pretty well verify who the young mothers are. The faint blue circles under their eyes tend to give them away. Then, when I ask mothers of babies under four to identify themselves, the hands they raise are the limpest, tiredest hands in the world.

Maybe you're like the mother I talked with recently.

She had been unable to have children, so her doctor prescribed the fertility pill. "Look at me now," she said in mock horror. "Suddenly, I've got *four* babies under four!" I seem to recall she had four circles under her eyes rather than two.

The Fatigue Syndrome

Being weary emotionally as well as physically seems to be a disease with young mothers. Fatigue is the factor that makes most of us doubt our abilities, our sanity, and even our degree of spirituality.

Both our daughter, Laurie, and daughter-in-love, Teresa, gave birth to baby boys within two months of each other this year. It was Laurie's first and Teresa's second child. One day I overheard Laurie asking Teresa:

"How long am I going to be this tired?"

Teresa's answer was not at all surprising. "Forever," she sighed.

When I was in my early twenties with two babies under four, I needed only one word to describe my life, *fatigue!* I've never been that exhausted before or since those days. As a young mother I remember feeling worn out beyond belief, and I truly believed I would never feel rested again in my life—and that fatigue was *forever.*

The first awful effects of fatigue occurred a few weeks after my first child was born. When I described my symptoms to my friends, they just smiled and said, "Oh, that! It's just 'after-birth blues.' You'll get over it." My feelings of depression were to be treated as if they were a short-term mental problem, which, given time, my mind would outgrow.

I learned much later that "postpartum battle fatigue" has been recognized by doctors since 1875 as a distinct, but generally benign, disorder that affects a large percentage of new mothers. It's also not all "in our heads," but results from a combination of emotional *and* physical factors.

The emotions and the body go through very radical changes during pregnancy. It is no wonder that immediately after giving birth, when we've abruptly lost as much as twenty pounds of baby and fluids, with the hormones at a very low level, and possible thyroid deficiencies, postpartum blues really hit us. The apprehensions and responsibility of caring for an infant loom before us, and we're at a loss to explain our feelings. We are profoundly overcome. One moment we cry, the next, laugh, and then we find ourselves talking gratefully of how glad we'll be when the baby sleeps through the night.

It's always precisely at this point that some forty-nine-year-old lady like myself comes up to you and feeds you two concepts that utterly gag you.

First: "This is the *best* time of your life!" Then she adds snidely, "You'll just hate it when they get to be teenagers!"

When my daughter-in-love, Teresa, was told this, she said to me, "If *this* is the best time in my life, why am I always crying?"

I had to remind her that women who make these comments are making a statement about *their own lives* and *their own babies,* who are now teenagers. Such an appraisal of life has very little to do with the young mother they are talking to.

Second: "This stage of life will go by very fast. Why, in no time at all the baby will be grown up and married!"

Right. Partially. I say this statement is *partially* correct because *my* babies *are* grown. But when you are living at this stage, with *your* babies, it's extremely difficult for you to see ahead even two years, much less ten or fifteen. Telling you that this time will go quickly is a little like saying, "If you wish hard enough on a star, someone will come in each week and clean and wax your kitchen floor commercially at absolutely no cost."

You are positive this child will never be five years old. Those babies of yours will never toddle off to kindergarten, and you're sure you'll be *forever* knee-deep in diapers, formula, and fatigue!

I've given both Laurie and Teresa this timely Scripture reference. (I'd engrave it on their foreheads if they'd let me.)

> And let us not get tired of doing what is right, for after a while we will reap a harvest of blessing if we don't get discouraged and give up.
>
> Galatians 6:9 TLB

The Pressure to Achieve

In addition to a general tiredness that runs through young mothers like a low-grade temperature, there is the subtle and overt pressure to be an achiever. The general idea is for women to excel, to work outside the home, to develop interests in other things, and to get involved in projects both in the church and in the community.

The suggestion to get out of the house and be fulfilled *never* comes at a worse time.

Ten years ago, sociologists and psychologists said that a child's character development is set by the time he is five years of age. Then a few years back, others moved it up and said, "No, a child's character is pretty well set at age three." Now, still other studies have narrowed it down to a year and a half. One study even said there was evidence that by the time a child was six or seven months old, he *knew* if he was loved or rejected by the way parents, adults, baby-sitters or whoever, changed his diapers, fed, or handled him.

If these studies about babies have a shred of truth in them, then I believe that the suggestion to "get out and do something for yourself" is not fulfilling anybody. On the contrary, it *loses* two people at least—the mother and the child.

I'm teaching Genesis right now in my Wednesday-morning Bible study, and we have been learning that one of the major differences that God made between the animals He created and mankind was that He gave mankind a conscience. God made mankind (not animals) responsible for *their* actions and responsible to others.

In those early months and years of your child's life, nothing can fulfill your total person as much as giving yourself to the immediate "Tender Loving Care" of that precious gift.

The problem with our society is that we want instant results, instant self-gratification, which will produce instant rewards. And raising a baby is never done instantaneously. It takes years to grow that baby into an adult. Hang on, you *are achieving*. It may take awhile to see it, but it is happening. It's just hard to wait twenty years.

When my babies were under four, I was not a born-again Christian, so there was the first snag. That's not to say that a mother who is an unbeliever cannot be a good mother. It's just that most of us, especially me, need all the help we can get. In those days I was not calling or depending on the Lord. The outside voices were loud and persistent and easy to hear. The pull to get women "outside" the home was as strong and as unchangeable as high tide.

My husband, Dick, was just out of the army, new on his civilian job, and finances were very tight. The message to be an outside-the-home achiever began to get to me. I succumbed and did possibly the dumbest, most ridiculous thing I've ever done in my whole life. Actually, to date, I've chalked up several large, well-noticed mistakes, but this one definitely reached an all-time high.

I took a new job.

Now wait, let me state right here and now, this is *not* a put-down of working wives and mothers. To work or not to work is a *very* personal decision, and must be made by you, your husband, and the Lord. I am not qualified to discuss the economics of your life, nor is it any of my business. All I'm saying here is that in the early 1950s, for *me* to give into the pressure and take a job with two babies under four was the height of stupidity.

I'm sure you'll see why. The job I took was as a sales-clerk in a toy store for a dollar an hour. Out of that hour's pay, I paid a baby-sitter fifty cents each hour she took care of Rick and Laurie. Topping that, I had to buy new clothes and shoes, and I took a taxi the four miles to the store because there was no bus service or second car. The job put us financially into the "red," and if there was some sort of emotional fulfillment achieved, it went right past me.

Each night I'd come home to cranky, tired, and very dirty babies. The house looked as if it would qualify for federal aid, because it could easily have been identified and declared a disaster area. Then there was that inevitable moment when Dick would walk in the door and recite the familiar husband's litany "What's for dinner?"

I never knew whether to scream, cry, or burn the place down! Worst of all, I had no idea that much of the horrendous mess around me—the bad scheduling, grumpy husband, and crying babies—had been created by me . . . or rather, by the lack and absence of me. And not once did it occur to me that the pitifully small profit my job paid once in a while was hardly worth all the effort.

At that transition time of my life, I'd have sold my half of the kingdom for five minutes alone in the bathroom without any little person asking, "What are you doing?"

There's good news and bad news about having babies. The good news is that God gave babies to young women, because He knew that they could not only take it, but that even if they made mistakes and blunders, they'd survive gloriously. The bad news is that by the time you've recognized the effects of fatigue, corrected some of your mistakes, developed a carload of patience, and actually matured in wisdom, your newly found insight is merely hindsight, and you're too old to have babies.

Every once in a while, I hear an older woman say, "I'm sorry, but I certainly don't identify with you, Joyce. I *loved* having babies. I wasn't tired all the time. I didn't find it confining or boring, nor did it rob me of my time for myself." At times like this I hold back my urge to flippantly comment in return, "Oh? Tell me, how long have you had this problem?" because I know that this lady, when her babies were little, probably had help—spelled H-E-L-P. Either she had a live-in mother, maid, English nanny, or a husband who quit his job to raise the children.

Very few mothers look back on those early days of motherhood and say with smug satisfaction all over their faces, "It was a ball! I loved every minute of it!"

Of course, hindsight is marvelous, and I can't help but wish I'd known then what I know now. I wish someone had pointed out the terrible toll fatigue was taking on me and had persuaded me to take daily naps without feeling guilty. I wish Dick and I had come to some kind of agreement that one of us would clean up the supper dishes while the other one gave the babies their baths and put them to bed. After all, we shared in *making* the babies. We should have shared in *caring* for them after they came. I wish, too, that someone had challenged me to choose far more carefully my priorities. But then, would I have listened?

Youth, inexperience, and a sincere belief that no one else has ever been in this kind of hot water, are some of the problems of young motherhood.

This is one of the first changepoint times at which a tired young mother tends to think, *Ah,* when *my babies are finally sleeping by 7:30 P.M., potty trained or off to preschool a few hours a day,* then *I'll have some time for me, and I'll get some rest.*

However, most changepoints are trade-offs, and we find the when-and-then concept is a hollow promise.

The Making of Mistakes

I was terrified of making a mistake in raising our babies. I read everything I could, talked with other mothers, including my own, and then found out much later, that mistakes are part of growing. I even found that I didn't need to feel guilty about the wrong choices or the wrong decisions I'd made. In fact, around the age of forty, I learned that it was all right to experience failures and that to "blow it" with your children or your mate was pretty routine stuff.

Eve was probably the first woman to beat herself with her own whip. She felt the first searing hurts of motherhood. Believe me, when her son Cain murdered his brother Abel, Eve was the first to say, "What did I do wrong? How could I have failed so miserably in training these boys?" She probably went to Adam and cried, "How could this have happened? We fed them the same oatmeal, we lived under the same tent, and we taught them the ways of God. I don't understand what went wrong. I didn't go out and get a nine-to-five job in the local store, and you didn't spend time away from home climbing the corporate ladder—*yet we've failed!*"

Neither Adam nor Eve had read the Bible or Dr. James Dobson's books, nor could they phone up their parents and ask, "What did you do?" They were simply the world's first parents. We can only imagine the frustration and guilt both Adam and Eve felt the day of their son's death.

I wonder how long it was before they realized that with all their hearts, they had done their best in raising their family? When did Eve first understand that the murder was not of her making or even her responsibility, but was Cain's *choice?*

I believe, as Eugenia Price has written, that Adam and Eve came quickly to grips with accepting their son's murderous act because they remembered their own sinful disobedience to God.

We are responsible for training our children with the best of our hearts and minds, but mistakes, failures, genuine disappointments, and a child's choice may change things drastically. They're part of life, and I've found that it helps to *plan* on their coming to pass!

From time to time, young and weary mother, you are going to yell the wrong response, attack when you should be still, lose any semblance of self-control, and make a first-class mess of things. But take heart! God is in control, even though you're probably too tired to notice, and best of all, He's growing you into a special mother.

Without sounding like a forty-nine-year-old Pollyannatype woman, believe me when I say I know how God works. I know how He shapes and molds His clay children, and if you trust Him right now—babies and all—you'll not merely live through *this changepoint,* but later you'll look back and shout, "Well, what do you know? I *did do* some things right, after all!" And it will come to you loud and clear that God was right in there all the time.

The Training Wheels

Our Bible tells us to train up a child in the way he should go, and when he is old he will not depart from it. (*See* Proverbs 22:6.) As I look back on that verse in connection with raising our own children, I realize a few significant things about this Proverb.

First of all, my responsibility is to train this child as I think *God* would have me to do. I'm to function much like those training wheels put on either side of a two-wheel bike. Remember them? They are not welded on for permanence. Rather, they are fastened in such a way that when the child is more accustomed to riding and keeping his balance, the extra wheels are taken off.

Motherhood includes making godly choices for that child until he is old enough to make his own. Training includes counting on God's granting divine wisdom on a *daily* basis.

Second, I am *not* responsible for the *final outcome.* My responsibility is only in the training.

Third—and this isn't a terribly spiritual point, but it needs to be said—Proverbs 22:6 never says *exactly* how old the child will be when he'll come back to his early training. In some cases, it could mean he'll be eighty-four years of age. But again, *this* is a problem but not our major responsibility, and God *is* a *faithful* God. Our part is to obey Him and to be godly mothers.

Notice I didn't say anything about being a perfect mother or a supermom, just wise in the Lord. And believe me, being a wise woman has very little to do with your age, IQ, or education. It has everything to do with how well you listen to Him.

But when you're tired beyond explanation, and you're sure you'll spend the rest of your life cutting up someone else's meat, how do you *really* know if what you're doing is right? You don't. It may take years for you to see any concrete evidence that you've been a godly mother. So hear this:

All you have is today! This moment. And as tired or filled with feelings of failure as you are—stop a second and be still. If you listen very closely, you'll be able to hear the still, small voice of the Holy Spirit, and you'll hear things like, "My child, this is the right way. You made the right choice today. It may not be a popular one, but it's the *right* one." And when you're really listening (because the Holy Spirit never yells), you'll hear His whispering, and your conscience will be stirred. A gentle conviction will prod you out of a potentially bad area and into the right one.

My granddaughter, April Joy, broke a rule at her house the other day. My daughter-in-love, Teresa, caught April in this fractured rule. Then, because Teresa had given birth to Richard Andrew just two months before and the fatigue factor was high, she just let loose with a barrage of shouting and scolding at four-year-old April. Finally, after Teresa had calmed down, after discipline had been administered, and after April's tears had been dried, Teresa had her usual make-up talk and time of setting things aright again. The conversation went something like this:

"April, do you know why Mommie had to punish you?"

"No."

"Well, you broke the rule. That's why."

Sensing that April was still angry about the situation, Teresa asked, "Are you mad at me?"

"Yes," April said soberly.

"But how could you be mad at me? I didn't break the rule—you did!"

Then April said evenly, "I'm mad because you yelled at me, and I'm going to ask God to take the yell out of your face."

Teresa said the soft voice of the Holy Spirit hit her with an incredible blow of conviction. The child was not angry over being punished—it was deserved—but she was hurt and angry about the personal injury of being yelled at.

Here Teresa had been trying to train her child in obedience, and was correct in disciplining her for breaking a rule, but she had lost her self-control (one of the fruits of the Spirit that identifies us as believers), and had carried out the action of discipline with a great deal of unnecessary shouting.

Instantly Teresa said, "Okay, April. You're right about my yelling. Let's pray."

April responded simply, with no malice, forethought, or anger, "Dear Jesus, please take the yell out of Mommie's face, and bless my kitty, Honey. Amen."

In the seemingly endless changepoint of her life right now, with two babies under four, the Lord was very special to Teresa that day. And what's really marvelous is that same helpful, whispering voice of the Lord that reached Teresa can reach through your fatigue, your mistakes, your failures, and even your babies' crying. He can, in His gentle, unobtrusive way, lead, guide, and give wisdom as you *train* up your children in the way they should go.

Take heart, for as unbelievable as it may sound now, it really is only a snap of the fingers from diapers to tuxedos and wedding gowns.

Your babies will grow up—and so will you—with plenty of changepoints along the way.

Recommended Reading

"A Moment for Mom," chapter 7 in *Dare to Discipline* by James Dobson, Tyndale House Publishers, 1970.

My First Three Hundred Babies by Gladys W. Hendrick, Vision House Publishers, 1978.

"Mom and Dad, Meet Your Child," chapter 1 in *You and Your Child* by Charles Swindoll, Thomas Nelson, Inc., 1977.

3
Changepoints . . .

The Children Are Off and Running

The potential of a child is the most intriguing thing in all creation.

ROY LYMAN WILBUR

Not long ago at the grocery store where I usually find most of my speaking and writing material, I stood behind a young mother and her son in the checkout line.

The boy's two front teeth were missing. He was jumping, hopping, shadowboxing, and, in general, was a picture of perpetual motion. I *knew* he was six years old.

Do you have a child between the ages of five to twelve? Then you know exactly where this mother was coming from. I imagined she was exhausted from her chauffeuring duties, the part-time job she held, the Sunday-school class of three-year-olds she was teaching, cooking and cleaning, wifehood, and all *that* entails, and now she was hurriedly trying to finish her shopping. Like all of us, she was horrified to find everything—from a can of soup to a loaf of bread—nine cents more this week than last. Mentally, all during her shopping, she concentrated on computing ways of cutting costs. By the time she'd done the

41

actual shopping, answered forty questions from her son, disciplined him three times, and maneuvered her un-pushable cart to the checkout stand, her general nervous system was not too stable.

A couple of times in my over twenty years of grocery shopping, I've seen a mother go totally berserk at the checkout stand. Each time, I've rushed supportively and lovingly to her aid because, while I've never gone that public with my hysteria, I am desperately familiar with the problem.

The mother in front of me, this day, did not come com-pletely unglued. Instead, she just released all her frustra-tions and tensions by flinging an ancient, yet ridiculous, question at her son.

Trying to get him to hold still while she locked eyeballs with him was quite a trick, but finally she managed, and as she grabbed one shoulder, she yelled, *"Why don't you stand still?"*

The question was not the type to be answered, but it did slow him down momentarily. I remember thinking at the time, *No kid his age has the slightest idea of what "still" means!* In fact, during the five-to-twelve years, they are more active than two cups of popcorn in a hot pan.

A New Perspective

If life at your house is bursting with activity, it may really be getting to you. If you're sure you can't stand one more slammed door, one more "race" through the living room and hall, or one more meal with little feet kicking each other under the table, it's probably time to change your perspective. Plan a little trip.

Go to your nearest hospital. Pick the ward that's filled with the seriously ill children. The thing that will probably strike the deepest in your heart when you take even a quick glance at the children is their apathy, their pale, quiet personalities, and their unnatural stillness. The experience will thoroughly chill your blood.

The only movement in these children's wards or rooms comes from the activity of the doctors and nurses. The children themselves lie strapped down with needles and tubes connected to every conceivable vein. They seem to hover between the never-never land of life and death—in an eerie, solemn silence.

Very quickly you understand just how marvelous it is that your child is filling your home and your heart with his nonstop activity. Forevermore you'll remember the parents of those hospitalized children. Those are parents who would *love* to see their child respond in some way—*any* way—much less talking, running, or hopping about. And you will go home to hug that noisy boy or that ever-busy girl and thank God for their *aliveness*.

Enjoying, Encouraging, and Enhancing

If this is the time in his life that your child spends every waking moment wiggling and squirming—enjoy it. All that excessive movement probably only means he's healthy and quite normal!

This is also the age when you may find yourself surrounded by self-proclaimed experts in the parenting business.

There is nothing wrong with listening to solicited and *un*solicited advice, or reading all the books and articles you can find. But listen and read with one ear open to the Holy Spirit's still, small voice. Examine the things you hear and read in the context of *your life in Christ*—not someone else's. Then *act* on what you've heard or seen as you believe the Lord would have *you* respond.

My kindergarten report card, carefully preserved in a scrapbook by my mother, still clearly reads, "Joyce has a lovely voice, but we are teaching her to sing softly."

Now, from the age of three, my mother had taught me to project my songs with all my lungs, heart, and soul. To read a report that someone was shushing me up was a cruel blow to her. She wasted no time, but marched off to my school. In a calm but strained voice, she explained that the teacher would do no such thing.

As far as music went, from that point on, my mother stepped up her encouraging words, and I continued to sing in a very unfettered way. Looking back on that time now, I think that had my mother gone along with my kindergarten teacher, I might have missed what was to be a special musical part of my life later on.

My mother wasn't always this motivated or in tune with the Holy Spirit. Long after I'd grown up, I discovered that she had second thoughts about the way she raised her children. So, I asked her if she would have changed anything in my childhood. Almost instantly she said, "I would have listened to all the women in Dad's congregation who advised me on your upbringing. But then, before I did anything, I would have laid everything before the Lord and asked what *He* wanted me to do."

Recently a young mother described the note written on her six-year-old son's report card. It stated that, as parents, they really ought to try to curb or tone down some of their son's noisy enthusiasm.

The mother said to me, "I was about to follow the teacher's advice, when I took a good look at each of our four boys. Suddenly I realized that this six-year-old was the only one of our children who had any enthusiasm. To turn him off or tone down that bubbly personality of his would be completely wrong. The other three boys were all shy, quiet, and very retiring. We *needed* this live wire at our house. So I told the teacher we were going to allow him all the freedom in the world to be as enthusiastic as he wanted to be, because our whole family could definitely use the lift!"

Bravo—wise mother! She was examining her son in context with their whole life and listening to that still, small voice of the Holy Spirit. Consequently, she was at her best to enjoy, encourage, and expand her child's heart and mind.

Even now, as I write this book, I want the words and illustrations to be simply guidelines. I hope to produce thought-provoking ideas and to help you hear the Lord's voice relative to your own situation and needs.

I'm aware that God speaks through His Word, His people, books, and even music. Beautifully, He uses all this to bring solutions for our problems and healing for our hurts. But the *exact* causes of action or the advice I've found to work in my life may well be shaded differently for me than for you.

Because we have been made exquisitely different and original, there simply are *no pat answers* and *no patterned solutions* for problems that arise.

So while it's very right to read and listen to others, always come back to square one, which is, "Lord, what do *you* want me to do?"

Remember the frenzied mother at the checkout stand in my grocery store? Her first question, "Why don't you stand still?" was followed by a second question. It was even better than the first! By this time, she'd reached the end of her fuse, and she sparkled like a firecracker with, *"Why don't you grow up?"*

I know the reason I laughed right out loud standing in

that checkout line was because I saw myself! I'd yelled that same question more than a thousand times to my own children. And, as I recall, almost every time I asked it, we were either at church or in the grocery store!

The Process of Becoming

"Why don't you grow up?" is another of those unanswerable adult questions. For there stands the child, doing exactly that—growing up!

The problem is that it takes twenty years to grow a child into an adult. Actually, for some kids it takes twenty-five or thirty years to see any maturity set in, but basically, we are talking about a twenty-year commitment. The process of becoming takes its own sweet time! No amount of wishful thinking will speed up the timetable, and it's our impatience that can nearly wreck our children's lives. We live in an "instant" age. We want instant gratification, instant growth, and instant results, and when it comes to our children, we want instant perfection and instant obedience. I know this because of a painful personal experience.

I can teach any child how to play the piano. It's all done simply by using patience as the tool. You sit down with the child and point out three notes—C,D, and E—on the keyboard. Over and over again, you say in a gentle, loving tone of voice, "Now, this is C. This is D, and this is E." Then you show him the notes on the music score and you say, "This is the same C and D and E as you have down here on the piano." Next lesson. Same as the first. You just keep going over it, lesson after lesson, until one day the child says, "Oh, I know where C is—it's right *there!*" And he's right.

When Laurie turned eight years old, I jammed her down on the piano bench and announced in my most severe tones, "It's time. So now you are going to learn how to play the piano!" Her bottom lip was already quivering, but I ignored her feelings and plunged ahead with, *"Now this is C, and this is D, and don't you forget it!"*

After two weeks of my screaming, and her crying, it dawned on me that I'd *never* be able to teach Laurie to play anything if I was going to attack it as a drill sergeant-mother. Coming to my senses, I sent her off to Ruth Calkin, and in due time, Ruth succeeded very well where I had failed miserably.

I had impatiently demanded instant perfection and denied the "becoming process" to take place when it concerned my own daughter. This is one changepoint of my life I wish I could redo. Hindsight is brilliant. I wish I'd had a little of it back then.

We spend much of our time as mothers shouting, "How many times am I going to have to tell you to pick up your clothes, brush your teeth, feed the cat, turn off the TV, and so forth?"

The answer, of course, as Dr. Henry Brandt told me so many years ago is, "Oh, for about fifteen or so years." And then he planted this little kernel of thought in my brain: "Who better than you, Joyce, to ask these questions over the years?" Yes, who better than me? And who better than you? Who could do it with more love than we mothers? No one!

I remember visiting a marvelous Sunday-school department once. As the proud superintendent took me to the various classrooms, I became aware of the teacher-student relationship in a new way. I found that by just observing for a few minutes, I could tell if a teacher had a child of her own in the class. Her sweet, patient, gentle instructions and teaching went to all the children but one. To that child, she almost snarled, "Sit still," "Be quiet," and, "Let someone else talk." I knew exactly which child was hers.

The teacher was demanding instant obedience and mature perfection from her own child, when she'd never dream of asking for it so bluntly from the others.

It simply *takes time* to grow, and no one time of growing is any more important than another.

Now, during this becoming process, especially when your child is between the ages of five to twelve, there is one other factor that highly colors things. It's called:

The Age of Gullibility

This is the time of life when children are totally gullible. When kids are junior highers, they don't believe a thing *anybody* says. When they are full-blown teenagers, they only believe their peer group. But, from the ages of five to twelve, they positively believe everything they hear— particularly what they hear from their parents, their family, and their teachers.

Webster's defines *gullible* in a very negative and distasteful way. The meaning is given as, "easily deceived, cheated or duped." So, I use this word cautiously, yet deliberately, for I want to impress you with its importance.

As parents we have the very powerful responsibility of programming our children's minds during these vulnerable years.

This child, during the age of gullibility, absorbs ideas and soaks up moral and spiritual values like a sponge. He is quickly impregnated with goals and dreams. In fact, often what he is to become in the future is set and formed in his heart and mind at this point. *He believes everything,* so he is easily impressed, easily influenced, and easily molded.

Why am I making such a big thing out of this word gullible? Because in the negative connotation of the word is the exact place we parents blow it!

We begin instilling positive character and moral and spiritual truths in our children, but the negative remarks, the critical comments, and the way we prematurely pounce and pronounce judgments often negate our well-intentioned training. The negative part stays forever with the child.

Unfortunately, when he grows up, he tends to forget all our positive nurturing and is more likely to remember our negative outpourings.

Dorothy Law Nolte has written the original (and the best) words about how we program our children.

A child that lives with ridicule learns to be timid.
A child that lives with criticism learns to condemn.
A child that lives with distrust learns to be deceitful.
A child that lives with antagonism learns to be hostile.
A child that lives with affection learns to love.
A child that lives with encouragement learns confidence.
A child that lives with truth learns justice.
A child that lives with praise learns to appreciate.
A child that lives with sharing learns to be considerate.
A child that lives with knowledge learns wisdom.
A child that lives with patience learns to be tolerant.
A child that lives with happiness will find love and beauty.

Perhaps at some time you have read this list (or one like it) and thoroughly agreed with its principles, but you have never compared it to *your* language in the grocery store or *your* response in daily life situations.

Maybe you did do that quick mental comparison and left it at that—simply an intellectual exercise. You never took stock of *your* words and actions.

You may never have done anything about the infighting between your children, nor have you set forth the no-knock policy. Since brothers and sisters have sibling rivalry and your house can turn into a combat zone, you need to see who it is in your family who is *always losing.* Most often it's the child in the five-to-twelve-year age bracket, and it comes at a time when he or she *desperately* needs to win—at least once in a while—for he is in the age of gullibility.

Here's a quiz. Don't worry. No one is going to score your paper or share your responses, but answer these with bare-boned honesty.

	No	Yes	Sometimes
Do you reward your child with a verbal or physical hug when he does something well?	___	___	___
Do you believe your child is aware of your family's spiritual and moral values?	___	___	___
Do you express, verbally or by touch, your love to your child after you have disciplined him?	___	___	___
Do you apologize to your child when you have made a mistake?	___	___	___
Do you take some time during the day to really listen to your child?	___	___	___

Whatever a child hears or feels during this gullible time in his life, he puts into his "computer." It determines what kind of an adult he will be—what he will strive to achieve, and what he will feel about his own self-image.

My brother, Cliff Miller, can vividly remember the exact moment, and one person who was responsible, when his self-esteem was crushed almost out of existence during his gullible years. His sixth-grade teacher said, "Cliff, you are so dumb! Why don't you become a dropout, go home, and watch Popeye on TV?" The remark killed all my brother's incentive to learn. It was years later—and after his experience as a marine medical corpsman in Vietnam—that he finally began to realize he was nowhere near "dumb." He came home to pick up his education, enroll in college, and later become dean of students at Seattle Pacific College. Cliff is a gifted man, but during his gullible years, one thoughtless remark nearly destroyed him.

Call a child "stupid," "brat," "monster," or tell him over and over that he does "the dumbest things," and he will live up to precisely the level you set. We need, as parents, to even watch the pet names we call our children. Sometimes we think because we joke or kid around when we use the nicknames of "runt," "ding-a-ling," or "little punk," that the child *knows* we are kidding. Why take a chance?

I was blessed to have a mother who continually told me I was special. Verbally she said things like, "Oh, Joyce honey, I can hardly wait to see what God is going to do in your life." She continued this stream of encouragement into my teen years, even when I had turned her off and was well into my ten-year rebellion. Nonverbally, she listened to me as I poured out the mundane and childish feelings of my heart and without words gave me what can only be termed "the approving looks of love." She left little doubt that someday, she *knew,* I'd be transformed from a caterpillar into a colorful and special butterfly. She did this not only for me but for my brother and sister as well. It's always been a sorrow to our family that she did not live long enough to see all those hoped-for dreams come true in her children. Without question I am what I am today because of the things my mother programmed into me during my gullible years.

Not too long ago I briefly shared my dentist's waiting room with a young couple and their seven-year-old son. As we sat there, the boy discovered a pile of children's books. Methodically he went through them, picked the right one, and waited for a break in his parents' conversation. When his mother finally turned to him, he asked her to read to him.

Then, more for *my* benefit than his, she said loudly, "Why, I'm not going to read you anything! You're a big boy, and you can read your own story. You know very well how to read!"

Inwardly, I flinched with pain for the boy, for I remembered the exquisite joy of being read to when I was a child. I was also flooded with warm memories of my own reading to Rick and Laurie. Reading aloud is a priceless way to program your love into children's hearts and to stretch their minds in the process.

The boy didn't say anything. He just turned, put the book back, sat on the chair, and soberly folded his hands. I was just going to say, "Here, I'll read the book to you!" when the nurse came in and said the doctor would see them.

What followed broke my heart. Without one word to the boy, both parents immediately got up and went through the office doorway. No verbal assurance of, "We'll be right back," "Come with us," or "Wait here." Just nothing.

Their son jumped off his chair and ran to the door. I'll never forget what he said. "Daddy, please don't close the door. Please leave it open," he pleaded. "Don't close the door, please, Daddy." He knew they were not going to take him with them, so the next best thing was leaving the door open. His father gave the short explanation of, "They want this closed," and shut the door firmly in his son's face.

The boy stood by the door for a long moment. Then he ever so lightly touched the doorknob, decided against opening it, and in one quick flurry of steps flew out the outer door to the street.

Almost instantly the nurse came out and asked where he had gone, and just before she disappeared out the door to get him, she explained, "When his parents were here before, he left, and we found him four blocks down the street trying to hitch a ride."

She brought him back, gave him a book, and told him his parents would be out soon. But the boy never smiled, looked at the book, or moved. He just stared at the closed door.

What has taken me several paragraphs to describe took only moments to act out. I found myself unwilling to believe what I was seeing and hearing. The sequence of events was begun and finished before I could respond, but I have relived this family's words and actions in my mind's eye many times since that day.

Over and over I have wondered to what extent his emotions were crippled that day. What kind of an adult did he decide to be in those moments? It's hard to tell, but even though it was the briefest of encounters, I'll always remember his soft voice saying, "Daddy, please don't shut the door." I wonder, too, how his gullible little mind will handle that in the years to come.

The minds of your children and mine are like the finest

computers on the market today. Their minds' ability to record and store information is phenomenal! We find that from the ages of five to twelve, we can program them— for better or for worse—beyond belief, simply by our words and actions.

Robert Louis Stevenson once wrote: "I am glad that in the springtime of life there were those who planted the flowers of love in my heart instead of thistles." The gullible years of our children's lives are the perfect seasons for planting flowers instead of thistles.

My sister, Marilyn, once told me that God had offered her very sweet advice about child rearing. He had said, "Marilyn, I am helping you to raise Christy Joy, and as long as you *obey Me* and seek *My direction,* we will *participate* in this task together."

It is reassuring to remember that as mothers we don't have to struggle without wisdom during the changepoint times of raising our gullible-age children, for we have a God who *participates* in our parenting.

Recommended Reading

Preparing for Adolescence by James Dobson, Vision House Publishers, 1978 (book and tapes).

Too Big to Spank by Jay Kessler, Regal Books.

Help! I'm a Parent by S. Bruce Narramore, Zondervan Publishing House, 1972.

Home: Where Life Makes Up Its Mind by Charles R. Swindoll, Multnomah Press, 1979.

4
Changepoints . . .

Thirteen Going on Thirty

I was sobbing into the phone. I was filled with one-fourth despair and three-fourths rage.

I shouted, "She's only fourteen, but she's driving me bananas! Furthermore," I wailed, "I'm turning in my mother button. I quit! I'm not going to be a mother anymore."

Dick's voice at the other end of the line was calm. (But then, why shouldn't it be? He was at the bank. I was home!)

Quietly he began to pray, "Dear Jesus, it's us again. And you guessed it—it's about Laurie. Now her mother's had it, so we come to You. Give Joyce the wisdom, the patience, the sense of humor, and the watchful eye of a hawk in regard to our darling daughter. Be especially real to both of them in this moment. Soothe their fragmented spirits and help both Joyce and Laurie to hold on for another six or seven years."

With a husband and a prayer like that, I had no choice. I pinned my mother button firmly back in place.

THE IMPORTANCE OF STAYING SANE
(Written while living with our teenagers.)

If the changepoint time of having babies is inundated with fatigue, and the changepoint time of raising adolescent children means constant adjustments and cautious communication, then the words which describe the changepoint time of living with teenagers may be called—*utterly devastating.*

One distraught mother of teenage twins admitted, "I *almost* wish they were back in diapers." Then she added wistfully, "Things seemed so uncomplicated then—it was just feedings, changing diapers, and doing huge loads of laundry . . ."

A young man, now in his late twenties, describes his teen years as "the pits, the absolute pits!"

Some dear friends of ours could hardly believe their ears when their recently turned-teenage daughter wailed, "I'd like to run away because I'd get adopted, and then my parents would love me!"

At the very best this changepoint time is frustrating (for parents and kids); but, at its worst, there is probably no pain quite like it in all the world. The teen years do not suddenly pounce on us out of nowhere—unless you find yourself in the unexpected role of a stepmother—but, for the most part, even though we've read books and heard others talk about this changepoint, we never seem quite ready or prepared for it.

We expect our children to progress in an orderly fashion—from infants to children, to adolescents, and then slowly, out there in the future sometime, to teenagers. We become, and rightly so, so involved with each stage of every changepoint that *whoosh*—the years run together and blur before our eyes.

One morning, it seems, we go from listening to our baby gurgle and coo to hearing that same baby clamor for his or her driver's license, and we are shocked to find that fifteen years have slipped right past us!

Let me go back for a moment to our first "baby" days.

Dick and I had been married almost a year and a half when *the* most perfect little boy in the whole world came into our lives.

Richard Blake Landorf, whom we instantly and ever since have called Rick, was blond-haired, blue-eyed, and blessed with a calm, eager-to-please temperament. He cried only when hungry or wet. He met each day with gentle cooing and shy smiles. He quickly won our hearts.

When Rick turned two—the age of the terrible twos I'd heard so much about—he bypassed the "terrible" part, and those years were the terrific twos for all of us.

A quiet "uh uh" from me, and Rick retracted his hand from the coffee table. A shake of my head, a lifted eyebrow, or a cautioning word from his father commanded Rick's ardent obedience.

By the time our little son went to school, we were feeling more than a little smug as parents and were pretty sure we had the market cornered on child rearing. Rick's grammar-school teacher called me in for one of those parent-teacher conferences and simply gushed on and on about our delightful son. I preened my feathers like a proud mother bird.

By now my husband and I were Christians, so we claimed Proverbs 22:6, "Train up a child in the way he should go: and when he is old, he will not depart from it." For us—with Rick—the promise worked. There were no heavy adjustments, no adolescent traumas to speak of— Rick just grew up.

The closest thing to trauma happened with Rick when he was twelve and refused to take baths. Even that was short-lived, because when he turned thirteen he saw a girl, and somehow that inspired him to quit the no-bath nonsense.

During our son's first year of high school, my husband read Rick's report card and tamely suggested, "Ah, Rick, I think you can get better grades than these. . . ."

Rick shuffled off to his room saying, "Yeah, Dad. I guess I can. I'll give it some more study." And with that brief exchange, Rick's grades came up the next semester and stayed there as we knew they would.

Other adults talked about the problems of disciplining children who were by then taller (and in some cases smarter) than they, but for us, disciplining Rick was just a simple matter of setting the rules.

During this changepoint of my life, I was the soloist for the First Baptist Church of Pomona, California, where we attended for almost twenty years. I remember sitting in the choir loft watching Rick, who was seated up in the balcony with his friends. If the gum chewing, talking, or laughing got out of hand up there, I had a set of hand signals that warned of my impending wrath. The system was simple. My index finger along the side of my cheek

meant, "I don't care *what* you're doing. Cut it out!" A
second finger meant, "We both know what the third signal is, so this is your last warning."

I never got to carry out the third step. That consisted
of Dick or myself getting up from wherever we were,
going up the main stairs to the balcony, and merely sitting
like a stone statue beside Rick and his friends. Oh, how I
would have loved the dramatics of that! Can you imagine
anything more horrible to a teenager than having his
mother or father sit next to him and his peer group? Such
a plague!

Rick always shaped up on the second signal, and his
behavior (and ours) was pretty predictable. As parents we
began to take an unreasonable amount of pride in our
"methods." After all, weren't we "training our child in the
way he should go?"

As I look back on our attitude at that time, I realize
nobody is as rigid and spiritually dogmatic as a very
young, immature Christian who has no experience to
temper and balance his spiritually enlightened intelli-
gence.

Dick and I were beginning to think that this business of
dealing with teenagers or coping with the rebellions they
often experience was highly overrated. We certainly
didn't relate or identify too much with parents who were
wringing their hands over their kids.

Fortunately the Lord knew our pompous beginning
from our humble ending. He knew, too, that one day,
after I'd learned a few formidable lessons, He'd let me
speak, write, and have years of praying with parents over
their teenagers. Knowing all that and more, the Lord
especially did not want me to set myself up above other
parents. Nor did He want me to tell people all about our
calm, balanced approach to disciplining Rick. But, most

certainly, the Lord did not want me to look down my spiritual nose and smugly say to parents, "Train up a child in the way he should go—like we have—and when he is a teenager he will continue to be simply wonderful."

So the Lord gave us Laurie.

Darling, beautiful Laurie . . . the blonde, blue-eyed joy of our lives who, on the eve of her thirteenth birthday, went from sweet to sour like a quart of milk left out on a hot summer's night.

Did you know every family has a Laurie? It's true. Now that James Dobson's book *The Strong Willed Child* is out and being widely read, a lot of people claim *their* child was the model for that book. Not so. He wrote it for *all* of us.

As I recollect, even from birth Laurie kept us, if not in a continual state of upheaval, at least on the edges of our seats. She was an Rh-blood-factor baby and survived two complete blood exchanges at birth. Then, at ten months, she was hospitalized with a serious sinus infection, which damaged the nerves in her ears and impaired her hearing. Early on, though, we could see she was a survivor. Any other child would have given up, but because of a tenacious, strong will she hung on. (I'm so glad she did!)

In Laurie's early years, we coped and fumbled along as best we knew how. Oh, that I could redo those years with her, knowing what I now know. We asked ourselves, "How can a child so sensitive, so creative, and so enchanting have her mind so utterly set in concrete?"

Both Dick and I took furtive glances at Proverbs 22:6 and our Laurie. We reasoned that God wouldn't break a promise, so in her fourteenth year *we* felt *we* must be doing something wrong. Most of all, we didn't know exactly what breed of child we had.

Here was Laurie, a slim, willowy teenager, and none of

the pat tricks, discipline routines, or loving confrontations that we had used with Rick were working. Dick and I supposed that all we had to do was to treat her as we had Rick, and then her teen years would be the same piece of cake Rick's were. Right?

Wrong.

We were like the Christian parents in Joy Gage's excellent book *When Parents Cry,* who erroneously expected that Proverbs 22:6 was not only a promise, but a *guarantee,* that children properly trained would never rebel.

As parents, Dick and I took all the responsibility for Laurie's behavior, and when she began to show all the classic signs of rebellion at fourteen and fifteen, we took on a truckload of parental guilt.

In a chapter entitled "Train Up a Child or Control a Life?" Joy Gage tells of reading the entire Book of Proverbs in one sitting. In red she underlined each verse that spoke of the teenager's responsibilities. With a blue pen she marked all the verses which clearly spoke of the *parents'* responsibilities. Her findings? (I wish she'd done this study ten years ago!) She found that there were four times more verses dealing with the teenager's responsibilities than there were for the parents' responsibilities. Mrs. Gage concluded, "Proverbs clearly holds the parent responsible for the training of *children.* Just as clearly, the book holds the *youth* responsible for many of his actions."

I wrote in a previous chapter that Eve was probably the first mother to take a guilt trip because of one son's killing the other. It was not Adam or Eve's training, or even the lack of it, however, but rather that *Cain* chose to do what he did, *after* he was no longer a child.

Hindsight now gives me this wisdom. It seems that the biblical concept of child rearing tells us to be very picky about rules and training procedures when our children are little. Then we are to gradually release the youth into freedom—gradually letting go of the rules and ending up in a consultant position to our adult sons and daughters. *That's* training up a child in the way he *should* go.

My friend Ken Poure, executive director of Hume Lake Christian Camps, agrees with me on the order of training. In fact, he has said in his meetings and seminars that whenever parents *reversed* the order of being restrictive in the early years and relaxing the rules during the teen years, there was nothing but family conflict. Years of counseling had proved the biblical principle over and over again.

Hindsight *is* great, isn't it? If I had the chance to go back and do our family's life all over again with our two teenagers, here are some of the things I'd keep in mind.

What's happening is as normal as the turning of the earth.

When Laurie turned fourteen, she *hated* everything about anything, and she *loved* everything about anything. Got that? What I mean is, she had absolutely *no* middle-ground attitudes or thoughts; no middle place of emotions, and no balanced spectrum of behavior. She was simply incredibly high or desperately low.

It was normal.

Laurie continually said "yuk" about my hair and my clothes. However, in this case, we were even. I hated her parted-down-the-middle hair which, while squeaky clean, nevertheless hung on either side of her nose. She criticized my funny underwear, and I was equally horrified that she wore no bra.

It was normal.

If I fixed chicken for dinner, Laurie inevitably wanted hamburgers. If I made hamburgers, Laurie wished we'd have tacos, and on it went. Over everything. We seemed to always be in the opposite corners of each and every issue.

It was all a very normal time.

If you had told me this was very par for a teenager's course—that it was normal—I'm not sure I would have believed you. I would now.

Next, after realizing that the frustrations of living with a teenager *are* normal, take a deep breath and relax. Then consider this: *You* may need to develop a change of attitude. "Me?" I hear you shriek. "What about my kids— *they* need a change of attitude far more than I do!" That's true. But, for now, try this attitude change on for size.

By all means, develop a sense of humor.

If you don't already possess a sense of humor, you'd better rush right out and get one because, darling, harassed mother, things tend to get worse before they get better, and now is the time when you're going to need as much fun in your life as possible.

Perhaps, in the dim recesses of your mind, you remember having a sense of humor. Well then, resurrect it, fast! Or, maybe you *never* thought life was too hysterically funny in the first place, and now that you've got teenagers, you're quite sure life has no funny bone. Having a sense of humor is not measured by how well you tell a joke, how clever you are with a pun, or how quick you are with one-line comebacks. It's an *attitude* of life, and it's the ability to not take your present circumstances too seriously. Granted you may know some women whose sense of humor may be more developed than yours, but *having* one is the important thing here.

While I was shopping with Laurie the other day, she

pulled a folded newspaper cartoon out of her wallet. "Remember this, Mom? You gave it to me right after I got my driver's license." The cartoon showed two girls talking to their dad. One girl says, "Cathy got her driver's license today—can we borrow the car to see if her license works?" The folded cartoon is a memory that was part of Laurie's development of her own sense of humor.

Actually, I've been cutting out appropriate cartoons and sending them to friends and family for years. I even do it for myself. There's a cartoon on my refrigerator right now, and it shows a bedraggled housewife at the front door. A man with a briefcase in hand is saying, "Hello. I'm from the Red Cross. I understand you're having a dinner which is an absolute disaster."

Now, that may not be funny to you, but when I think of the mashed sweet potatoes sitting atop their pineapple rings spilling all over my kitchen floor in front of fourteen guests, or the time I ran out of food while serving the Bob Sheppard Chorale—I think the cartoon is totally delightful.

You may not be as witty or gifted in humor as Erma Bombeck, but I'll tell you, looking for humor in everyday situations, relaxing a bit, and chuckling over the mood swings of a teenager will definitely help you to keep sane another six months—at least.

Just as crying is a good tension releaser, so is laughing, but you may have to look for a reason. So *do* look—it's there!

Remember my mother's comment about nobody in Washington caring a whole lot about my skinned knees? It was her way of teaching me not to take myself too seriously. It was good training because each time I've fallen and skinned and bruised my ego, or had a shattering time with family or husband, I've taken the problem seriously, but not without a positive note of hope and good humor. More times than not, there has been something humorous about my plight—even if I had to wait a few hours or days to really see it.

As you work on developing or exercising your sense of humor, you'll need this next skill.

Learn to cultivate the ability to communicate verbally and nonverbally.

Most families nowadays have a huge stockpile of words at their house. Fifty years ago children were seen but not heard. Mother and father, or one parent, did all the talking. That has changed. Boy, has that rule changed! Everyone is speaking up, it seems. However, the sad thing is that very little is being said.

We do not *mean* what we say, nor say what we mean. So most times, while we have lots of dialogue, there is little understanding.

The authors of the book *Teenage Rebellion,* Truman E. Dollar and Grace H. Ketterman, summed up the typical type of communication in the home when they wrote:

> When a father tells a frustrated son, "I understand, I have been there," he is probably wrong. Their worlds are different, and it has greatly increased communication failure. The modern obsession of parents with careers, life goals, and television has further reduced conversation between parents and children.
>
> Parents are listening to words, but the different frame of reference has cut off understanding. Parents must now listen with ears, eyes, and heart. Unless a child believes he is getting through, he will stop trying.

I know a girl who did exactly that—stopped trying to communicate—and she remembers the exact moment when the flow of words ended.

She was fifteen, and a teacher at school had just explained some of the mechanics of designing and building the California freeway systems. One day, while riding on a Los Angeles freeway with her parents, the girl began to enthusiastically share what she had learned. Each time she pointed something out or gave an explanation about the road or approach ramps, her father retorted, "I knew that a long time ago!" Several times the mother asked him to listen to their daughter, but he cut her off too, and in the end the girl just stopped talking. Years later she pinpointed the day on the freeway as the beginning of their inability to talk or communicate on anything. Her father had heard her words, but was not listening with his eyes or his heart. He missed the genuine wonder at the workings of a giant freeway system. His I-know-it-all attitude killed his daughter's joy and drowned the fire of youthful enthusiasm. They never really talked after this encounter, and the father never suspected the cause. He simply listened from his frame of reference, and in doing so cut off all understanding and finally closed the door of communication.

It's one thing to hear our children; another thing to understand what they are saying.

I believe our teenagers are at a time in their lives when more than any other time, they desperately need to talk to us, their parents. They are frustrated, angry, and crying to be heard—but sometimes we are too busy with jobs, too wounded in our own struggles with life, or too apathetic to make the effort to really hear them.

When Rick and Laurie were young and we found the schedules of our lives beginning to race pell-mell toward a frantic series of deadlines, I began to believe that I was never going to "hear" my children. If I missed one day of talking with them, I missed out on a "fabulous day," or a day that was "the pits," or "who broke up with whom and is now going with so-and-so." So I did a time study on our kids. I tracked down what time of day had the highest point of communication in it. Guess when . . . fifteen minutes after they come home from school. So, I made myself available around that time each afternoon.

I was fortunate with my speaking career, in that I could speak for a luncheon but be home before the kids (sometimes just barely), or I could take an evening banquet or service. But mostly, I was home for them to spill out, "You'll *never* believe what happened today, Mom!" More often than not, I *said* very little, but learned a lot about hurts, victories, and the level of my teenagers' moods, attitudes, and self-esteem (or lack of it). It was always *very* revealing.

Some of the nonverbal communication techniques we used were touching, kissing, laughter and tears, and the continual practice of writing notes.

Still today our grown children embrace us and are dedicated to the process of teaching their little ones to "give Grandma and Papa hugs and kisses."

A woman told me of raising her children without any "emotional display" of affection. With tears in her eyes, she told me how wrong that had been. She backed her statement by adding, "When our oldest son was killed in an accident a few months ago, I realized that the only time I'd patted his hand or touched his face since he'd been three years old was at his funeral—and then he was hard and cold and it was too late for him to know about the love I'd kept to myself all these years."

Besides touching, we had a great deal of laughter at our house, especially at dinner time, and mainly because the dinner table was *the* time to be together as a family. But while there was laughter, we also wept together. Certainly, there have been hundreds of times of laughter to only a few times of weeping, but the tears have been there, and the loving communication that flowed with them was rare and precious.

Another rule of the house, from the time the children hit first grade and really began to print, was to let everyone know where everyone else was by always leaving a note. We are still leaving notes, sending cards, and writing out our communiqués through the mail. I've kept all the notes, "thank yous," birthday cards, and so forth, that our children have written since their childhood. What a treasure. And now that Dick and I are alone, I'm always delighted by opening up the mailbox and finding a card or a love note from our kids or my husband, addressed to me. The lady who comes in and cleans for me once in a while is still talking about the day she came and discovered that in every room of the house there was a fresh rose in a vase and a note from Dick to me that said, "I love you. Welcome home." (I'd been gone two days at a seminar.)

But the most important thing to do in regard to communicating has to do with praying.

After your teenager's name, put his peer group at the top of your prayer list.

Psychologists are not agreed on too many things, but in this one area they are unanimous: Nobody and no thing influences your teenager like his friends! Peer-group pressures affect different kids in different ways, but they are all influenced by them to *some* degree. Count on it.

It only takes one member of the peer group to push your teenager under the sea of life and drown him. That's the bad news—the good news is that it only takes one member of the peer group to keep your teenager's head above water!

"The significance of peer pressure cannot be overemphasized. It is rarely the cloak-and-dagger drug pusher who introduces a young person to his first drug experience. Almost invariably this is done by his 'best friend.'" So say the authors of *Teenage Rebellion*.

How true. So, if I could find a way to light the next words in this line with a neon sign, I would, because *we must pray for our children's best friends.* It may save their lives.

In a chapter coming up, I'll tell you about a girl named Gayle, whom we had routinely prayed for because she was Laurie's best friend, and you'll see how the "bread" of our prayers—when cast upon the waters—came back to us. Those years of praying for Laurie and her friend were instrumental in sparing Laurie from making a decision that could have cost her, her life.

There is no finer gift for a father and a mother to give to their children than unitedly praying for them and their friends. Believe me, you and yours—we and ours—need all the godly creative help we can get!

Here's a little checkpoint list to see how you are handling these years of frustrating changepoints.

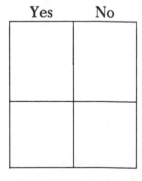

	Yes	No
1. Do you shift gears in your tone of voice from mother-to-child talk to mother-to-young-adult talk?		
2. Are you releasing new freedoms each year as your teenager has a birthday?		

3. Are you listening, not just with your ears, but your eyes and heart also?

4. Are you communicating non-verbally with touching, laughter, tears, and the writing of notes?

5. Are you praying not only for your teenager, but for his friends as well?

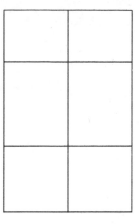

This teenage changepoint time can be, as I pointed out at the beginning of this chapter, utterly devastating, although I pray not. As parents it's important to not fear the changes which take place in the lives of our teenagers. File away, somewhere in your heart, that rebellion and a straining of relationships is done with much less trauma when a person is fourteen than when he or she is forty or fifty.

I pray that the thoughts of this chapter have given you the loving encouragement you need as you deal with your teenager who is going on thirty.

Recommended Reading

Teenage Rebellion by Truman E. Dollar and Grace H. Ketterman, Fleming H. Revell Company, 1979.

When Parents Cry by Joy P. Gage, Accent Books, 1980.

The Hurting Parent by Margie Lewis with Gregg Lewis, Zondervan Publishing House, 1980.

Home: Where Life Makes Up Its Mind by Charles R. Swindoll, Multnomah Press, 1979.

5
Changepoints...

The Super-Ten Mother

*God has encouraged me to venture beyond myself
into his territory—the realm of the impossible. The
impossibility of finding and sharing delight and joy
in this situation is really over my head. The waters
run deep and fierce, but I am swimming!*

GLORIA HOPE HAWLEY

I've been fantasizing about a perfect super-ten mother ever since Bo Derek became the world's symbol for female perfection. Is there such a person—a super-ten mother?

As I was thinking about Bo Derek, I realized that somewhere in my head I had my own preconceived ideas of what a super-ten mother should be. I saw the woman in my mind's eye like this:

1. Her face is a symmetrical vision of beauty, and her flawless figure—curvaceous, yet wondrously slim.

2. Her clean and well-shaped head of hair is always "bouncin' and behavin' " between casual and glamorous.

3. Her clothes, which she sewed, are neither plain nor pretentious. And even if you catch her in her jeans and sneakers, she is a picture of studied grandeur.

4. Her outside beauty is matched by her inside sparkle and teachable spirit.

5. Her inner calm never erupts into a fiery volcano—even when her little one throws small toys in the toilet.

6. Her responses to daily domestic crises are controlled, with just the right amounts of peaceful negotiations and quoted Scripture.

7. Her husband, best-looking man in town, stands up with awesome respect whenever she enters a room; positively raves about her culinary skills to others; and

refuses to be seated with someone else's wife at dinner parties.

8. Her children are normal enough, but extremely bright and beautiful. The bumper sticker on the back of their bicycles reads, "Have you hugged your mother today?"

9. Her relatives, even distant cousins, have only the finest things to say about her, and their loyalty is completely unshakable!

10. Her pastor and church body of friends give her yearly mother-of-the-year awards. She is practically famous at church and the PTA for being a perfect super ten.

If you're thinking, *And Alice walked through the looking glass into Wonderland*—I agree. I realize that list of super-ten qualities is a fairy tale in today's big, bad, real world.

It occurred to me when I was reflecting on my list of requisites, that I'd *never* met a perfect-ten mother. Occasionally I'd been with a woman who scored maybe five, out of ten, points, and on rare chance meeting I'd found a woman who seemed to have seven out of ten; but, I began to think, there was no such thing as a super-ten mother. Right?

Wrong!

There really *are* super-ten mothers. In fact, this year alone, there will be around one hundred thousand women who will qualify for the first time for the super-ten-mother title. They are all around us. I was simply measuring up tens from the wrong checklist of ingredients. It took a mother-and-daughter banquet to give me a true picture of a real "ten."

I wasn't late for the church banquet, but I came in just as the three hundred or so women were seated. The lady in charge was relieved to see her guest speaker, and she hurried me down through the maze of tables. Off to the side of the stage she stopped, pointed to an empty chair, and said, "We are not having a head table this year." (I was grateful because I've developed an intense dislike for head tables. They cut off communication, because everyone has to sit lined up in a row, like pigeons on a tree branch.) I tensed a little, however, when—with a flippant wave of her hand—she walked away saying, "I'm not going to introduce you to the ladies at your table because I know you're not shy!" I watched her go and thought, *I'll take assertiveness any day to plain old bad manners.*

The typical church-gymnasium table had four women seated at the sides and one woman at each end. I took the only empty seat, put my purse, Bible, and notes down, and said hello to the lady on my right. She mumbled something and then turned back to the lady next to her. Then I looked across the table but couldn't get anyone over there to catch my look, much less stop talking or introduce themselves.

The lady on my left, at the end of the table, was having a conversation with the lady across from me; so when I saw her pause to breathe, I put my hand on her arm and said, "Hello, my name is Joyce. What is yours?"

I knew right then that I had interrupted this century's most important conversation because, with a scathing look of disgust, the woman ignored my question and snapped, "Hello."

The salad was delicious, but it was an odd feeling—sitting at a table for ten and eating alone.

I consider myself a communicator and, as the chairperson suggested, I'm not basically shy; so my initial surprise about my table mates' lack of manners slowly boiled from frustration to pure anger. No matter what I said, I simply could not get anyone to engage in any conversation with me.

Somewhere between the salad and the main course, since no one was going to talk to me, and I had gone from anger to boredom, I began to study the lady on my left.

I didn't like her. On the Bo Derek scale of ten, she was a minus three. Her face, old and wrinkled, was further intimidated by a tired, rather nasal, voice inflection.

As I was cutting into the creamed something that was served over baked something, I broke into the lady's conversation and, nodding to the young woman across from me, I ventured, "Is this your daughter for tonight?" The older woman paused for just a second and then answered clearly, "I don't *have* a daughter," and resumed her conversation with the young woman.

What was I doing here? Idly I thought, *If I had wanted a disagreeable dinner hour, I could have stayed home and refereed a fight between Rick and Laurie, or I could have explained how I burned the casserole—again.* Any number of things would have been better than this.

A marvelously tempting voice inside of me suggested that I merely slip away from the table—no one would ever notice—get into my car, and drive home as fast as I could. I almost did—it would have served the chairperson right!

Then, ever so quietly, the Lord reminded me of Keith Miller's book. I'd just finished reading *A Second Touch,* and it was all about seeing people not through our own clouded eyes, but through the clear, loving eyes of Jesus —seeing them as Jesus sees them. I almost gagged on the vegetables because I was sitting adjacent to one of the most miserable looking ladies I'd ever seen, and even trying to see her as Jesus must see her was pretty impossible.

However, I was committed to being the main speaker for this banquet, and by now I was highly bored, so I took a tiny peek. Then I stared. (She didn't mind because she didn't see me staring.) I was positively fascinated. There sat the same, very same, woman who had been there all evening; yet, there were a number of significant changes in her face. I saw literally years of fatigue etched into that face, and I knew, too, that the soul beneath the face was enduring a painful crisis.

"Ask her about the blue circles under her eyes," the Lord seemed to say. I wasn't about to be that direct, so I touched her arm (the only way she'd look at me) and asked, "If you don't have any daughters, do you have any sons?"

She caught her breath and then fired at me, "Yes, I have one son. He's retarded, and has the mental capacity of a four-year-old. He's in the hospital, and he's dying. I don't want to be here, but I promised my husband I'd get dressed up and stay just for the dinner. Then I'm going back. Does that answer your question?"

I can't explain my feelings at that moment, only I do remember praying for the gift of wisdom and thanking the Lord that I'd read Keith's book and experimented with "looking at someone through the eyes of Jesus."

Touching her arm again, I said, "Tell me. How old is your son?"

"He's thirty-four," she answered stonily.

The blue circles, the fatigue, all the things on her face that I saw when I looked a second time, now made sense. For an instant I sat stunned, and then the Lord gave me an idea.

"Tell me," I asked her, as she pulled her arm away, "would you play a pretend game with me?"

"A game?" Her look was amused and skeptical at the same moment.

"Yes," I said, and then, before she could turn away, I plunged on. "Let's pretend that I am in the hospital. I have just had my first baby. I'm twenty-one years old, and suddenly my doctor and two other men I've never seen before come in. My doctor says they have bad news. My baby boy is mentally retarded. From all they can tell, he may some day achieve the mental abilities of a three- or four-year-old, but that physically he's in good shape and will probably live for thirty or forty years. I am stunned. The doctors allow no questions, and when they leave, a cold wave of panic covers me. I try phoning my husband, but he has just left the hospital and can't be reached. My folks are out of town, my friend is grocery shopping, and I can't find anyone. I'm desperate. Then you walk into my room. What would you say to me?"

The woman straightened up a bit, and rather impassively stated, glibly, "I'd tell you that God would take care of it all."

By now I was so involved with this whole experience that I didn't politely touch her arm. I *grabbed* it and thundered at her, "Don't give me any of those worn-out clichés! My baby's retarded, and I have to come up with some answers or I'll die! Now, what are you going to *honestly* tell me about thirty-four years of living with your son?"

The woman turned in her chair, really looked at me, and for the first time understood that I was serious. So, in thoughtful, measured tones, she began to put thirty-four years of God's faithfulness into words.

Quietly at first, she began to tell me about some of the immediate decisions I'd have to make. How I'd have to decide whether or not my baby's retardation would mean his staying at home or would require his being institutionalized. How I'd handle people's, and especially other children's, inhumane treatment and taunting remarks. About the time her son was five and invited to a birthday party in their new neighborhood—but was quickly sent home by the mother who didn't want a "crazy" child to spoil her son's party. How the Lord had specifically met her husband's needs through this son, and how every year the boy lived proved to be a rich, rewarding time of growth.

Almost glowing now, and quite beautiful, the woman assured me that her son was a rare and treasured gift from God. Even the whining, defeated tone of her voice was gone—replaced by tender, sweet, enchanting sounds.

But the real miracle that unfolded before my eyes was that this woman—worn thin by the impending death of her son, ungracious and rigid in her manner—softened, mellowed, warmed, and even began to glow. It happened as she remembered and recounted God's goodness to her and to her husband; and, believe me, she went from a "minus three" to a "twelve" as she talked.

She was still candidly sharing details and incidents about the joys and heartaches of her life when the chairperson of the banquet stood up and began a lengthy introduction of the speaker for the evening.

"I'm sorry," the woman whispered. "I've got to go back to the hospital. I'm not staying to hear the speaker."

"That's all right. I understand."

Then, at that moment, the chairperson said my name. The woman got up, did a double take from the chairperson to me, and asked cautiously, "You're the speaker?" I nodded.

"Oh, dear. I can't stay. I'm sorry." She shook my hand.

"I know, and that's just fine," I responded honestly. "I didn't come here tonight to be the speaker—the Lord wanted me to come to hear you, and it's been an experience I'll never forget."

She thanked me, took three steps toward the back of the hall, stopped, suddenly turned, and came back. "I just have one more thing to tell you."

I thought she was going to relate something more about her son. Instead, she looked straight into my eyes and said, "I love you."

I stood up, hugged her, and assured her that I loved her, too. How I managed to hold the tears back and reassemble my shattered emotions to go up on that stage to speak, I'll never know. Except that God allowed me to do just that, and He had let me see a woman—a true super-ten mother. She had been at her absolute worst and her most glorious best, and I've never been the same since.

If you have a handicapped child—whether the handicap is a mental slowness or retardation, a congenital birth defect, epilepsy, deafness, a speech defect, paralysis, a disfiguring birthmark, crossed eyes or blindness, or some disease that has crippled or deformed the body or the mind—I see you as a super-ten mother . . . a special woman of God.

It is possible that one hundred thousand women will become mothers of handicapped children this year. Will this be your year? Your changepoint? If it is, I agree with my friend Chuck Swindoll when he says that God indeed has given you an extraspecial child. Handicapped? Yes! Special? Yes, that too!

A friend whose daughter is a teenager and a dwarf—a little person—said the worst thing that could ever happen to them as a family was to have an irreversibly brain-damaged child. However the very best thing that did happen was that they had an irreversibly brain-damaged child. That daughter is the delight of their lives, and I'll tell you, my friend is definitely a giant super-ten mother!

Seeing your handicapped child as God's special gift to you, without rebellion and an infectious bitterness within you—even understanding that you may never know the answer to the ever lurking question, "Why?"—will free you to be the very superspecial mother He has planned for you to be. You'll probably go from a one or a two to ten on the scale of motherhood in an instant!

This changepoint time of caring and loving this child,

of living your own life out may be altered or rearranged, but how you see yourself and your child will determine the quality of your existence.

Gloria Hawley, mother of two retarded children, wrote to all mothers when she said in *Laura's Psalm:*

Our family may be a little different from yours. But this is our design. My race course differs from yours; but it was marked for me, by the One Who was marred for me.

Jesus loved us before we could respond correctly, in love, to Him. He died and gave His all, for men who were dead and retarded spiritually. Can we do any less?

The arena is invisible to us, as are the standing-room-only crowds who fill it—but it's real. A cloud of witnesses who've gone before are watching. The opposing team is watching.

We are vulnerable and run the obstacle course in alien territory. We are finite, and subject to erosion of time. The very cellular structure of our bodies causes us to fluctuate and change. However, when our inner beings are founded on the everlasting and unchanging I AM— even occasional bedlam does not change the fact of Very God.

I must believe and be nourished and exercise in order to grow and do my job.

Someday the children, Laura and Craig, will be gloriously transformed in the perfection of God's Presence. They will come forth from their existence in this life as gorgeous butterflies emerge from the dark constriction of cocoons. They will be perfect and mature, having lived their lives on earth to the best of their ability.

How will I be revealed?

How will you be revealed?

Who's retarded?

Is your child handicapped or seen by the world as "less than perfect"? Then, take heart. For just as surely as that child has been given by God—he will return to God; and it will be no mundane, obscure thing, but the birth of an exquisite butterfly.

And in the meantime? What about the impossible changepoint days that lie between you, your child, and his or her transformation?

Let me turn you to my friend Gloria's words once more:

> All through the New Testament, Jesus asks, "What do you want me to do for you?" Oh, dear Lord, every day help me to believe and obey You! Constantly help my weakness of faith. Be my faith! Be my strength! Live my life today!
>
> Impossible?
>
> No; rubbing a lamp, or kissing a frog is impossible.
>
> All we have to do is accept the free and ultimate gift of unconditional love and eternal joy.
>
> All we have to do is tell Him about it, and trust Him. His specialty is impossible people.
>
> I know.

Dear super-ten mother, once—a couple of thousand years ago—a very young, completely bewildered virgin was told by an angel that she would become pregnant and bear a child. She voiced her first disturbing thought by bluntly asking, "But how can I have a baby? I am a virgin."

The answer, so right for young Mary, whose son, Jesus, would be handicapped by a sin-filled world in the most ultimate way, was right for you too, at this moment. For the angel calmed her fears and gave her glorious hope. He explained that the Holy Spirit would come upon her and that the power of God would overshadow her. Then, this precious promise: "For with God, nothing is ever impossible . . ." (Luke 1:37 AMPLIFIED).

The Holy Spirit, the power of God—these are your secret weapons for this incredible changepoint; and, since nothing is impossible for God, it's no wonder you're a super-ten mother!

My list of ten qualities for a super-ten mother describes the mother of a handicapped child in this way.

1. Her face, though lined sometimes with fatigue, is beautiful and dominated by sparkling eyes because she really sees her child as a gift from God.

2. Her hair is sometimes messed up, but that's because she lets her child playfully run his fingers through it. She also takes him to the clinic each week instead of taking herself to the beauty shop.

3. Her clothes are neat, in style, and colorful. No sackcloth and ashes treatment, and no mourning dresses worn, because she's not grieving.

4. Her outside loveliness is only outshone by the ever-present beauty of Christ within her. She's radiant and has done a good job of developing her sense of humor.

5. Her inner calm gives way at times to inner frustration, but then she steadies herself because she knows God has a plan for her child and for herself.

6. Her responses to daily domestic crises are not always logical, practical, or even spiritual. However, she is determined to treat her handicapped child as naturally and fairly as possible, for she knows his happiness and self-esteem are at stake here.

7. Her husband may not be *the* most handsome man in town, but he possesses such a gentle way and caring spirit that he is irresistible to her. Their commitment to God, each other, and their child is astounding.

8. Her other children are smarter than anyone else's. From their parents they have learned how to make

allowances without pity for their handicapped brother. Loving, wholehearted acceptance of this special one is a way of life to them.

9. Some of her relatives do not readily understand or relate very well to her child. But this knowledge does not distress her for she knows she, her husband, and her other children are, by the grace and strength of God, carrying on with confidence in God's plan.

10. Her pastor and church body of friends have sometimes dismayed her by what they have said or done in regard to her child. But she understands their well-meaning hearts and takes comfort from women like Gloria Hawley and Dale Evans. She knows God understands her commitment to this changepoint time, and she waits patiently for God to mature His people's hearts.

Now, this is a *real* list. So you see, dear super-ten mother, you are terrific!

Recommended Reading

Frankly Feminine: God's Idea of Womanhood by Gloria Hope Hawley, Standard Publishing, 1981.

Laura's Psalm by Gloria Hope Hawley, Impact Books, a division of the Benson Company, 1981.

Angel Unaware by Dale Evans Rogers, Fleming H. Revell Company, 1953.

You and Your Child by Charles Swindoll, Thomas Nelson, Inc., 1977.

Early Warning Signs, National Easter Seal Society, 2023 W. Ogden Avenue, Chicago, IL 60612. A free booklet in English and Spanish for mothers who suspect their child may have a special need.

6
Changepoints . . .

The Plan of God

Don't let the world around you squeeze you into its own mould, but let God re-mould your minds from within, so that you may prove in practice that the Plan of God *for you is good, meets all His demands and moves towards the goal of true maturity.*

ROMANS 12:2 PHILLIPS

This may be a changepoint time for you when the words of Paul, about God's plan, meeting all His demands and moving toward maturity, seem a little farfetched. Vaguely, you believe God *has* a plan, but "meeting and moving?" You're not sure.

Your confusion centers on the question: "To have, or not to have, children." And it's a heavy decision.

Many couples today—whether by prayerful and deliberate choice, or biological and/or physical limitations— are *not* having children.

You and your husband may have tried, but five or six miscarriages later you have given up. Or, perhaps you and your mate took a good look at the moral and spiritual decay in this world and firmly decided you were not about to bring any children into it.

Whatever your reasons—you are married, childless, and wondering what "the plan of God" is really all about.

This part of this book, then, is for you. I hope I can heal some of your wounds over this delicate question and focus your attention on the real message of Romans 12:2.

Whose Plan and Whose Business?

First of all, to *not* have a baby after one or two years of marriage gives family, distant relatives, and friends something to discuss over coffee or at reunions. However, should you go on and still not have babies after three or four years into marriage, the "discussions" turn into downright prodding, meddling, and hard-line judgments. The questions run from casual, "How come a nice young couple like you doesn't have children?" to attempts at humor, "Don't you two know HOW?", to direct and sticky, "Are you *ever* going to have kids?"

Actually, the truth of the matter is—whether you have children, don't have children, adopt them, or marry a man with six kids of his own—it's none of the business of the rest of us. It's *God's business.*

Yet so often we—especially those of us within the circle of believers—pry, interfere, and make verbal judgments in regard to the childless couple.

I suppose we come by this attitude naturally, because in biblical times it was a cultural and spiritual disgrace for a woman to be barren. Read about one woman's agony in Genesis 30:1 (RSV).

"When Rachel saw that she bore Jacob no children, she envied her sister; [Leah had already given birth to four sons] and she said to Jacob, 'Give me children, or I shall die!' "

Later, when she did become pregnant and gave birth to her son Joseph, Rachel breathed an enormous sigh of relief and declared, "God has taken away my reproach [disgrace and humiliation]."

Her reproach (which came from others), her disgrace (which was known in the community), and her humiliation (which she experienced to the point of wanting to die) would only be taken away by God's giving her a son. The family around Rachel, the community, and Rachel's own self-condemnation led to frustration and caused her deep despair.

It was all so utterly needless!

God's plan, had she known, called for not one son but two! However, Rachel couldn't put her confidence or trust into an unseen, unfelt God.

Like us, Rachel didn't *see* God blessing her womb, only Leah's, and in her heart she didn't *feel* that God would answer her prayers for motherhood, so she *assumed* God had no plan.

Rest assured, dear childless woman, if God wants you to have a baby, you will—one way or another. You who could never hold a pregnancy beyond a few months—will. You who *cannot* will adopt. And you who have neither of the above options, may end up becoming a stepmother, finding your life *blessed* with *instant* motherhood. But if you are to be a mother by God's plan—you will; so don't be impatient or let the world around you verbally squeeze you into its boxed-in mold.

Your decision on this, as I said, is none of our affair. Our response—as family, friends, and body of Christ is to *love* you. To love you, with no questions, no judgments stated, and no strings attached!

More importantly, you need to take a deeper look at God's purpose for marriage.

Only once in the Old Testament is God so concise about His views on marriage. There can be no mistaking His words when, in Genesis, we are told, "Therefore a man shall leave his father and his mother and shall become united and cleave to his wife, and they shall become one flesh" (Genesis 2:24 AMPLIFIED).

Notice—carefully—there is not one word about having children. The views on marriage expressed here talk only of two people becoming one, not two people becoming three or four.

Dr. Walter Trobisch uses this verse in his marvelous book *I Married You,* and points out that, "Children are a blessing to marriage, but they are an additional blessing to marriage." He goes on to say:

> Therefore when the Bible describes the indispensable elements of marriage, it is significant that children are not expressly mentioned. Leaving, cleaving, and becoming one flesh are sufficient. Full stop. Even if there are no children the one-flesh union does not become meaningless.
>
> The full stop means that the child does not make marriage a marriage. A childless marriage is also a marriage in the full sense of the word.

The Genesis 2 account is indeed talking about blessing the marriage of *two* people.

Also—I've always been fascinated with how often God uses a childless couple to work so beautifully with other people's children. I think of my own early years, when my dad was a pastor in Saginaw, Michigan. I was three years old and away from my grandmas and other relatives. It was a childless woman next door who gave me the brightest and most beautiful times of my childhood.

Every afternoon, after my nap, my mother would let me go next door to visit. The lady, whom I called Auntie, would bring out to her back porch a little green table with one little green matching chair, and I'd sit down to a feast of raisins and animated conversations. I never knew which I loved the best, the lady or the raisins.

Rollin and Ruth Calkin never had children of their own, yet Rollin was the Christian education director of our church for thirty years. The Sunday-school enrollment was to involve 2,000 people Sunday after Sunday. His wife and co-worker, Ruth, had hundreds of piano students (including my own two) who loved her dearly. That "childless" couple understood very clearly and very early in their lives, exactly what the plan of God was; and even though the plan did not mean children of their very own, it did mean a lifetime of teaching, counseling, and loving thousands of children. In fact, having no children of their own probably (because it was in God's rich plan) *enhanced* Ruth and Rollin's ministry.

Youth counselors and pastors, choir directors, missionaries, teachers, nurses, librarians—my list could go on and on—all of these vocations, when in the plan of God, can be enhanced by the childless couple.

Once you relax in Romans 12:2, look out—God may bless you with a thousand children! Tell that to your mother, who keeps bugging you about her need to be a grandma.

What About the Option of Adoption?

Perhaps you and your husband are unable to, or have, for reasons of your own, chosen not to have children. Prayerfully you have decided that with all the homeless babies in the world, adoption *is* a part of God's plan for you.

To you I say, "Bravo!" I really do hope and pray you take up the option of adoption. I can think of no people in the world better suited to adopt children than a man and woman who love God and each other.

Only eternity will tell the full story of what *might* have happened to that baby had he *not* been adopted by Christian parents. Parents who gave him God's unconditional love, nurtured him physically, mentally, and spiritually, and then released him as an adult to serve the Lord.

In my Bible study and in seminars, I have asked women who have adopted a child this question: "What did people say when they found out you were adopting?" Generally, the answers have been frustratingly familiar. They went something like this: "It's nice you adopted a baby (or child), but you can never know how a real mother feels until you've actually given birth."

Hog wash! Three times I discovered I was pregnant. And two out of the three times I reacted by throwing up my hands (and my dinner) and hollering, "Oh, no!" Fortunately, by the end of the sixth month I changed my mind, but not so with a woman who wants to adopt. She takes a flying leap at loving that child *long, long* before she's even sure she's going to get him. Her head start on motherhood eclipses mine in an instant. Also, according to friends of ours who have one natural child and one adopted—*there is no difference in their parental love for each child.*

Besides the tactless, unfounded response about a mother of an adopted child never really being able to know how a "real" mother feels, here are some of the other typical questions frequently asked of a couple who is considering adoption:

"Are you really sure you want to get involved with someone else's child?"

"If the baby turns out to be sickly or retarded, can you give it back?"

"How much did this adoption cost you?"

All of these questions are positively humiliating to the couple who has prayed and waited out the long procedures involved in adopting. All this couple needs to hear from us as they are "expecting their child" is, "Praise the Lord! Children are a gift from God, and we'll be praying that you become very special parents to this very special child!"

I just love it during a baby dedication at church when the pastor turns from the couple and their child, faces the audience and asks, "Do you pledge, before God, to prayerfully uphold this couple as they train and nurture this child? Do you promise to be supportive to this child in case this marriage is dissolved by death or divorce? And finally, do you see how very much this young couple needs the loving approval of this congregation—especially in times like these?"

When the audience's answer to these questions is a resounding yes—heaven records the ringing joy! And then the who's, what's and how's of this couple's adoption should be put to rest.

Not too long ago, I heard a young man talk about his parents. He had been adopted by them as a baby, and when asked if he would be interested in someday meeting his biological mother, he answered kindly, "Yes, I'd be interested in meeting her. She gave birth to me, and saw that I was placed in a good home; but those things in themselves did not make her my mother. While I'm grateful to her—still, it was my adoptive parents who sat up nights with me when I was little and sick; worried with me when things weren't going well in school; fed me—both physically and spiritually; laughed and cried with me; and shared my heartaches, disappointments, joys, and triumphs. They are my *real* parents."

Nobody, absolutely nobody, is better equipped, darling Christian woman, to be a mother to an adopted child than you! Even if you are on the foster-care mother program, and have babies and children for only a short time—you still have a portion of the mind of Christ, and that alone sets you miles ahead in the wisdom department. And who knows—since all children are only *loaned* to us—maybe this brief time with you will be the one and only time when this child touches base with the loving Lord.

Go to it, in all joy!!

The Cinderella Syndrome

I am admittedly a fan of the decent, yet highly creative, work of the late Walt Disney. He drew cartoons, made wholesome movies, and designed the most magnificent amusement park in the world. He endeared himself to me because he did all this work with his own two daughters in mind. No one, before or since, has come up with the inventive genius of Walt Disney and been able to utilize it in quite the same refreshing and wholesome way.

Having said all that, I do have to voice a less than enthusiastic opinion about one of his contributions to our present-day society.

When Disney and his staff portrayed the stepmother in the fairy tale of *Cinderella* as ugly, unfair, mean, and totally wicked—they gave the world a most distorted image.

Few stepmothers have had a chance, or been given the emotional climate to prove themselves otherwise. Women have gone into a marriage involving stepchildren with the "wicked stepmother" image so locked into everyone's mind that sometimes there has been very little chance to break out of the mold.

We are only now beginning to see a tremendous increase in remarriage and stepparenting, and it will continue to even greater proportions. Take a good look at some interesting facts:

1. One out of every five children in this country is the child of a divorce.

2. Eighty-five percent of divorced persons remarry within five years.

3. In the United States, right now, some 20 million adults are stepparents.

We must be wise enough to understand that given these statistics, there is bound to be an ever-increasing number of adjustments and problems facing stepparents and stepchildren alike.

Add those adjustments and problems to the "wicked-stepmother image" and you've got a pretty depressing starting point. It used to be said that the hardest job in the world was being a mother. But, after talking to a lot of women, I think I'll change that to say: The hardest job in the world is being a stepmother.

Here are a few suggestions I've gleaned from women who have gone through the stepparenting experience.

1. If it's at all possible, start your new family life in a new or different house. Feelings are closely entwined with a home or apartment, and to start in a new place helps to cut down on old feelings and begins to generate new feelings and emotions.

2. Watch out for the too-high-expectance syndrome. Don't expect instant love, instant involvement, and instant rapport with your stepchildren. A solid relationship takes time. Let love and caring for each other develop slowly. God's timing is rarely ours. Read the Old Testa-

ment's greatest piece on waiting, as found in the Book of Habakkuk.

3. Let the children participate and share their feelings in deciding what the stepparent will be called. Some children will have no problem with Mom, Mommie, or Mother—others will. First names may be the best route, or invented nicknames; but, whatever—get the child's input. It will speed up the adjustment time.

4. Basic to a good relationship is your ability to call your stepchild "my son" or "my daughter," especially when the child is under ten years of age. This may be difficult at first, but just as you must break away from the image of the "wicked stepmother," referring to your child as yours instead of stepchild, is a pledge of respect, and it helps to lift the child's self-esteem.

5. The tendency to go soft in the area of disciplining your stepchild is normal. However, it can be disastrous. A good way to begin is to let the biological parent do much of the disciplining, and gradually to share the loving responsibility. But, by all means, let all the children know there is only *one set of rules* for all children (mine, his, and ours) and that you and your husband are firmly and unitedly agreed about it!

Is being a stepmother really a tough, difficult occupation? You bet it is . . . especially in the early days of adjustment!

However, there is a great deal of hope here, and stepmothers all over the United States are quick to share it. It seems that most stepmothers admit that while family-life adjustments are harrowing, dangerous to their mental health, and often take years to accomplish—still—with the Lord's ever-present, ever-available strength and help —it's well worth all the effort!

I've seen these stepmothers with my own eyes and listened to them as they have shared their stories and their love for *each* of their children. Believe me, there is no such thing as a wicked stepmother—only fantastic women who have "enlarged" hearts and a capacity for loving like I've rarely seen!

So, the real message of Romans 12:2 is that you resist outside pressure from a godless world, and you let God remold your attitudes, reactions, and even opinions, from within. I know the plan of God for you *is* good so keep at it! It's worth it all!

Recommended Reading

Is There a Family in the House? by Dr. Kenneth Chafin, Word, Inc., 1978.

"Stepmothers Aren't Wicked Anymore" by Eda Le Shan, *Parents* magazine, June 1980.

You and Your Child by Charles Swindoll, Thomas Nelson, Inc., 1977.

7
Changepoints...

Soloing

*I was in the wilderness of my life.
I was a Gretel without a Hansel lost in
the woods. There was a wicked witch who
would eat me if I would listen.* In my
thoughts were my wars fought.

LAUREL LEE

This was written by Laurel Lee after she turned thirty, bore her third child, discovered she had Hodgkin's disease, and watched helplessly as her husband divorced her.

It seems to me that there are at least two kinds of soloing. The musical soloing, where we sing by ourselves; and life-style soloing, where we live, sing, or cry by ourselves.

The musical kind I've known about all my life. And—while this next statement may not be terribly profound—let me tell you: Soloing wouldn't be all that nerve-racking except for the fact that somebody is always changing the music. Each piece that comes along is brand new, each song has a change of tempo and pace, and each musical rendition brings with it its own challenge.

I'm not too sure that life-style soloing is all that different from musical soloing. For about the time you adjust to living solo and you're getting the hang of it, someone or something changes the music. The cadence is off the beat, the lyrics overwhelm you. What can *never* happen—*does.* In one fell swoop your song is a jumbled up bunch of discords and sour notes.

For twenty-nine years I have been duetting with Dick in marriage, so I don't know if I can readily relate with those of you in the soloing changepoint of your lives—or can I?

For at least twelve of those twenty-nine years of marriage, I have traveled, written books, talked, and listened to many thousands of women. I've done my share of fact gathering about soloing in life.

Many of those women are, for one reason or another, single. Some are soloing by their own choice; others, by uncontrollable circumstances, some by divorce, and still others by widowhood. But they are all living out this time in their lives on their own and by themselves.

The Aloneness of Soloing

Whenever I am asked to speak to a Sunday-school class for singles, a singles-only retreat, or a conference for single parents, it is always suggested that I talk about the problem that plagues the singles the most—loneliness.

Now, I know this is a viable and real subject for concern among singles; but I always have to smile a bit because truthfully, do you know who has the biggest problem with being lonely? *People* do! Persons from all walks of life and all different life-styles struggle from time to time with the feelings of loneliness. And of all the married and unmarried women I've talked to—very often the loneliest woman is not the one soloing, but the one duetting.

One letter from a married woman who has several children stated succinctly, "Every night I fix dinner for six, but I eat alone!"

All of us know about the chilling effects of loneliness. It's a cold, grey mist that filters in and around our hearts. You try turning up the heat or dressing warmer, but it isn't very effective in warding off the chill. It's a cold that seems to settle in the very marrow of our bones. Is there any way to protect ourselves or to insulate our walls so that we do not become rigid with, and frozen with, loneliness?

I believe so.

During my childhood I had much time alone. My brother, Cliff, was born when I was thirteen. I was leaving home for a Christian boarding school in another state. My sister, Marilyn, was born when I was twenty. I was leaving home to get married. So I was raised for the better part of the time as an only child.

My parents were heavily involved in pioneering churches. During part of my childhood, my mother worked full-time in an office. There were no strictly "family" vacations. Only trips to camp meetings and denominational conventions, or times when my father filled in for another pastor in a neighboring town. On rare occasions we saw relatives, and I had a chance to play with my dearly loved but seldom seen cousins.

We moved almost every two years until I was ten, so making and losing friends, continually changing schools, houses, and churches gave me a very real sense of aloneness.

I am especially grateful for those years and the lessons they forced me to learn. I look back on all that rootlessness, that aloneness, that continual state of upheaval, and realize God was teaching me the intricate and often obscure difference between being alone and being lonely. They really are two different concepts. And in the process of growing up—that early solitude became a good, reliable friend to me.

Richard Foster has beautifully described the difference between aloneness and loneliness in his remarkable book, *Celebration of Discipline.* I was delighted to read in the chapter on solitude these words: "Jesus calls us from loneliness to solitude." I'm so glad he didn't say Jesus calls us from loneliness to be the-life-of-the-party-type person. Funny, but the word *loneliness* takes on a new coat of paint when we consider replacing it with the word *solitude.*

Two thousand years ago, in the press of the Judean crowd, in the extreme stress of mounting pressures—Jesus just slipped away. He melted, as it were, right out of the scene. Where did he disappear to? *Into solitude.* No one went with him, not even his favorite three—Peter, James, and John. If Jesus needed the healing balm of solitude, how much more do we need it?

Famous celebrities often travel with an entire troupe of people. They are never alone. With them, always, is their entourage.

Jesus implied that not only was it all right to be alone, but sometimes it would be an absolute necessity to our spiritual, mental, and emotional health. The call to solitude breaks new ground in a world that insists, in order to be successful and whole, we have to be surrounded by tons of adoring, approving friends and loved ones.

Later, in Richard Foster's book, he defines *loneliness* as "inner emptiness," and *solitude* as "inner fulfillment."

I can really buy that! Inner emptiness is a preoccupation with "Poor-me-I-am-all-alone-and-so-blue." Inner fulfillment employs the attitude of "Wow-now-that-I-am-alone-and-Jesus-is-here-with-me-I-can-recover-repair-and-regroup!" The truth of the Apostle Paul's words to the Philippians, when he writes, "I have strength for all things in Christ Who empowers me . . ." (Philippians 4:13 AMPLIFIED) rings clear. When this Scripture is applied to the times of solitude, it becomes a powerful season of real growing.

Being alone in my childhood developed my ability to be remarkably comfortable in solitude—and only hindsight tells me how very important that aloneness was for me.

The solitude forced me, at a young age:

To invent games one person could play.

To read all kinds of books and then to revise them, in my imagination, into plays or movies.

To enlarge my love of colors by wearing down thousands of crayons in countless coloring books.

To give my undivided attention to piano practice each day. (I accompanied the children's choir and junior choir by the time I was ten.)

To make special times of being very still—times just to listen to the sounds of the world around me.

I never think of that childhood as being lonely. And I'm sure God used it all to prepare me for the times of aloneness down the road. It began to teach me the proper way of coping with the loneliness of being a woman, a wife, and a mother; the loneliness of grief; the loneliness of being a leader and a teacher; and the special loneliness of traveling, speaking, and writing books.

How practical God is in equipping us with just the right background, right experiences, and exactly the right peo-

ple so that we may understand the amazing difference
between loneliness and solitude.

The Choice in Soloing

Almost every time I hear my friends Joni Eareckson and
Ann Kiemel speak, I hear infused into their whole being,
their willingness to embrace solitude as a friend—and as
a result, they are survivors!

It's as if these two young, single women understand
clearly that they are *never* alone; and that out of their
soloing, God is producing marvelous fruit. I believe that,
more often than not, the fruit of the Spirit in their lives
has been planted and grown in the soil of their solitude,
during their quiet and private times.

I can hear your protest. "Wait a minute—that's just
dandy about Joni and Ann! What would you expect? They
belong to the beautiful-people set. They write, and they
are the women who are successful on the speaker's cir-
cuit. They have half the world paying court to them. Why
shouldn't they be victorious survivors?"

"Tell me, then, about *your* life," I ask, and I hear you
describe your time of soloing.

"I'm unattractive, plain, and shy. No one wants to be
my friend."

"I've never been past the eighth grade. I was married,
a mother, and divorced before I was nineteen years old."

"I've been taking care of my invalid mother and my
younger brothers and sisters all my life. I've no life of my
own, and I'm angry."

"I'm divorced and constantly hassled by my ex-hus-
band."

"I'm a lesbian and thoughts of suicide are never far
from my mind."

"I'm a widow with small children. What man would give me a second glance?"

"I'm a single parent and scared to death all the time because of all the financial, mental, and spiritual responsibility."

Before I talk about your soloing, let me go back a moment to Ann and Joni. Not only do I think that they understand the value of solitude, but I *know* they have chosen to accept their destinies (in Joni's case, paralysis, which does not go away), and God is constantly showing them the beauty of soloing.

"Beauty? What beauty is there in my solo?" you ask. Beauty, in *anyone's* life, comes painted in a sunrise of colors and is called acceptance and contentment.

Some of the most beautiful people in the world today, you may never have heard of. They've not written books, been on talk shows, nor are they household names. But they *are* beautiful and they are all *soloing*. I wouldn't want to walk in their shoes, live their lives, adjust to their traumatic experiences, go through their divorces, sustain their losses, or lose my husband, as some have. But there is a beauty in their lives that really shines. The glow from their heaven-sent contentment is simply breathtaking.

In her own unique way, Ann Kiemel has written of her decision to choose acceptance and contentment. It was not an instant and overnight arrangement between her and the Lord, but rather a process which tended to take fourteen steps ahead and nine back most of the time. In her book *Yes*, Ann tells about the up-and-down, in-and-out daily struggles and triumphs of the solo life. I love her honesty when she truthfully admits to times of longing for a husband, a marriage, and children of her own. She admits her humanness—so does Joni—and I'm glad they do. How awful we'd all feel if we felt that God had given Ann and Joni some special kind of gift or guarantee that meant they never had to deal with feelings, dreams, or heartfelt desires! I am highly amused when Ann relates the story of visiting her married sister, Jan. Her sense of humor is alive and well when she compares the choices open to her (where to hang pictures in her apartment or the decision to bake cookies at 2:00 A.M.) as a single woman, and those *not* available to her sister, who has to check with her husband. Most of all, I admire Ann's dedication to the Lord. For instance, more than once, and in the middle of a personal crisis time, Ann has chosen to really put God first—ahead of her desires—to honor Him, and not to succumb to the roller-coaster emotions of heart. Bravo, Ann!

The message here is that not only Ann had a choice, but all of us do too! We can moan and groan over our circumstances, analyze our emotions until we've left no stone unturned, or we can choose to follow the Lord's direction and accept the *now* of our lives, at this present moment.

Thousands of women are soloing in our world today— the beautiful ones are the ones who have *chosen* to accept soloing as God's plan for now. Acceptance followed by contentment are the flags that fly above them!

Paul was single, and his wisdom, borne out of soloing, has come down through the ages. I'm glad he was single! Actually, he would most likely have made a poor husband and father. Can you imagine Mrs. Paul being asked the whereabouts of her husband? She'd have to say, "Oh, he's off cruising the Greek Islands." Or, when his son asked if his dad was coming home soon, his mother would have to answer, "I'm afraid not right away. He's in jail—again."

Oh, dear. Enough of this.

Paul was a soloing expert. In his letter to the Philippians he wrote about being ". . . satisfied to the point where I am not disturbed or disquieted in whatever state I am" (Philippians 4:11 AMPLIFIED). And then, in that same letter, he tells how he has managed to live in times of plenty or in times of want. Also in the Amplified Bible, it's beautifully put when Paul writes, "I have learned in any and all circumstances the secret of facing every situation. . . ." It seems to me that he examined all the alternatives open and *chose* the way he would face every situation.

I wish Paul had elaborated on the word *secret,* but I think he did give us a clue when he mentioned *facing* every situation.

Before we can adjust to life, as it is for us, we have to *face* it. Verbally or nonverbally we have to admit, "This *is* happening." For instance, one of the most positive steps out of the valley of bereavement comes when a widow says firmly to herself, "My husband is *not* coming home from the office or from a business trip. He will *not* hold me or his children in his arms anymore. I will *not* be able to hear his laugh or tease him about his funny way of sneezing. He is *not here* anymore. I'll see him in Heaven, but *not* on this earth again."

By choosing to face up to this dreadful yet real fact, this woman can then go about adjusting her thinking, her attitudes, and her responses. She can begin to plan again. It's solo this time, and maybe that's brand-new to her after thirty-some years of marriage, but it's *the way things are.* She now has a choice. She can accept and adjust to learning the secret of being content, or she can withdraw from family, friends, and the world around her. She can even harbor bitterness until its odious festering eats away her inner soul.

Many people, not just those soloing, suffer from the debilitating malaise commonly known as the "When and Then" syndrome. It sounds like this.

When I get married and find Mr. Right,
  then I'll be happy.

When I have children,
  then I'll feel fulfilled.

When my church gets a pastor I like,
  then I'll get involved.

When my boss gives me a raise and I get some money,
  then I'll tithe.

When my divorce is final,
  then I'll be really free.

When I get my tax-refund check,
  then I'll buy a new wardrobe and be beautiful.

When I succeed in my work,
  then I'll get respect from my parents and others.

The trouble with the "When and Then" syndrome is that it forces you to live completely in the future. You miss today's new's and now's. Also, this kind of thinking sets your expectations too high and somehow—if you do find Mr. Right, if you do get a promotion, if you do succeed, et cetera, et cetera—the "then" is never what you dreamed it would be. You find yourself in the cold winter of disillusionment, and there you are shivering without a coat.

Someone has said, "The trouble with perfectionists is that they are never ready." Living continually in the future, with enormously high expectations, cripples you so you are never quite ready for the now's of your life.

Saint Paul wanted us to live in the "Now and How" of our lives, choosing to accept and being content with *whatever* state the now presents. The "Now and How" syndrome would read like this:

Now I am living alone.
How wonderful to know Jesus is *here with me.*

Now I am divorced.
How comforting to understand that God has not rejected me.

Now I am a widow. (A darling older lady—recently widowed—actually said this when I asked her to find something to be thankful for. She showed the practical side of God when she said:
How grateful I can be that on Monday nights I don't have to listen to Howard Cosell.)

Now I am a single parent.
How good it is to be assured that God is participating in my parenting.

Now I've lost everything.
How blessed it is to have the freedom of Christ to cry, feel broken, and know healing is on its way.

Now I am a woman—soloing.
How incredible of God to write Isaiah 54 as a love letter just to me!

The "Now and How" syndrome is beautifully expressed by Eugenia Price. I don't know where or when she said this—I found it among my papers on a scrap piece of pink paper. It reads, "The only direct statement of Jesus which is simple enough for me to comprehend when my heart is breaking, or when I'm discouraged or scared is: 'Follow me.' I cannot understand life because life is not understandable, but I can grasp, 'Follow me.' "

That is choosing to follow today. This moment. Not tomorrow or when it's convenient, but *now*.

Persevering—As a Single Parent

Parenting—as I have written before, in previous chapters—is, in any shape or form, at best, an exciting and blessed challenge. However, at its worst, it can be everything from merely ridiculously frustrating to overwhelmingly crushing. And while it's one thing to have a husband —especially one whose ideas, attitudes, and spiritual goals are the same as yours—it is quite another ball game to play the parenting game as a single.

According to a recent Gallup Poll, the divorce rate has doubled in the last ten years. If this trend continues, a conservative prediction indicates that almost half of *all* marriages will end in divorce. As painful as that statistic is, the next one is worse: Two out of every five children born in the past ten years will live in single-parent homes.

Listen to some of the statements made by single parents:

"I'm not going to make it. I'm just not. I can't be both mother *and* father to my children."

"The worst, the absolutely *worst*, thing about being a single parent is *all* that responsibility."

Now read this deeply touching letter. It's from a young widow with four children. Her husband died eight-and-a-half months *after* he sustained burns all over his body from an accident.

Dear Joyce,

    Well, he's gone. Ten days ago exactly. One week ago tonight we were attending the memorial service. It was a lovely service, everybody said, very inspiring. I'm sure it was. I was mainly trying to keep my three- and four-year-olds quiet. . . .

Everybody keeps asking how I am doing and I say "fine." Mostly I am. However . . . a great deal of the time I feel like Christmas tree lights. Ever try to get them untangled once they've made up their minds? No way. I keep trying to sort it all out . . . decide once and for all how I feel, but it's no go. I think, "You're adjusting beautifully." Why, I've even started thinking about my next husband.

And then I come down. I think, "Why did my husband do this to me? How dare he go and die, leaving me with four children?"

My dear Christian (not too helpful) neighbor just told me tonight that no one would ever want to marry a woman with four relatively small children. Bless her! . . . But then, how could I be so crude as to be thinking of another man. . . .

I have my best screaming fits in the car, where I hope and pray I cannot be heard. . . .

This young widow's letter, so open and so honest, is one of the healthiest responses to grief and being a single parent I've ever encountered.

It's very sad to hear the remarks of the body of Christ in dealing with the single person, the single parent, the widow, or the divorced woman. I know things are said by well-intentioned people who mean no harm; but, oh, the hurt they inflict is monstrous.

The woman who told my friend that no one would want to marry someone with four children did much damage, but basically she committed two no-no's. Number one, she put my friend in a box marked "Unfit for Marriage." And, secondly—and worst of all—she did nothing to show she knows *anything* about the character, mercy, love, or grace of God.

We, as the body of Christ, are even worse when it comes to the divorced among us.

At the beginning of this chapter, I quoted from *Walking Through the Fire* by Laurel Lee. She described this time of single parenting as the wilderness of her life.

Laurel wrote a sequel to that book and called it *Signs of Spring*. If you are a single parent, you will identify and relate with each of the 118 pages of this truly tender book. Laurel spreads out the life of a single, divorced woman with cancer, *and* three small children. She writes, "I wondered at God about my circumstance. Before words come pictures, and I saw a vessel on a potter's wheel. The sides of the clay were being pinched to create lines into its form. Pressure improved it. The way of surviving is to find meaning in suffering." Laurel was writing of the pain the newly divorced suffer from, and of its devastating effects.

Later, in talking with her mother about the newest changepoint of her life, Laurel wrote:

> My mother sat across from me drinking coffee. The interiors of some of her cups have a haze from their years of service. I watched her cigarette smoke as an almost invisible host moving between us. She told me a lot of people in the family have had cancer, but I was the first one to be divorced.
>
> A visit with parents is like a ball dropped to bounce in place. The momentum of greeting is its height. It loses altitude after the news is shared, and hardly clears the floor in admonitions.

Parents aren't the only ones who can't accept divorce. Children, relatives, and—as I just stated—many members of the body of Christ can't, either.

We get stuck on the *reason* for someone's divorce. Who filed first? Who walked out on whom? And a lot of other questions that compassionate Christians would consider none of their business.

The woman who is already divorced and raising children doesn't need one more judgmental opinion from us, the body of believers. And the woman facing the death of her husband, and single parenthood, doesn't need our helpful solutions and trumped-up remedies.

It's amazing how compassionate and merciful we are to someone who is ill with some dreaded disease . . . how we are supportive to prison ministries . . . and how willing we are to overlook and even forgive someone with a critical spirit. Yet, how slow we are to minister to the single parent, especially if she's divorced.

Laurel Lee wrote, "Religion that is pure . . . is visiting the fatherless children." About her sagging spirits, she wrote, "Depression was a garment that I couldn't take off. I tried to unbutton it all night with prayer."

Where were we—the hands, the feet of Christ, when she wrote those lines?

While I was doing a TV program on single parents for the Gary Randal Program out of Portland, Oregon—one of the women in the audience shared the following experience with us. She had been divorced for a year and had chosen to stay in her same church. She recalled that almost every Sunday friends of hers would hurriedly assure her that they were thinking of her and praying for her— then they'd rush off, leaving her with a hurried "Lord bless you" and a light pat on the shoulder. Finally by the time the fourth friend gave her the same impersonal little speech, she grabbed the friend's arm and fairly hollered, "Well, *that's not enough!*" Then while the friend stood in shocked silence, this young, frustrated, divorced, single parent asked, "How come when we were three people you invited us to your home for dinner? You took my child with you on some church outings. You phoned me often and acted as if you cared. Before the divorce, you always gave my daughter your daughter's hand-me-downs. But not now. Now that we are only two, you avoid me. And when you do see me, you brush me off with a quick greeting, a pat on the shoulder, and a bland, 'May the Lord bless you.' "

I was deeply touched and a little more than convicted. How many times have I been guilty of being hospitable and prayerful for those "couples" I know and love, but not "singles"?

Dr. Kenneth Chafin has developed a special ministry to the divorced, to the singles, and to the single parents. His 7,000-member church in Houston, Texas, is a lighthouse for the hurting single person, and I pray other bodies of Christ will band together and tackle this burgeoning problem. We need to minister to the real needs of the hurting singles instead of paying empty lip service.

In the Scriptures James says, "Pure religion and undefiled before God and the Father is this, To visit the fatherless and widows in their affliction . . ." (James 1:27 KJV).

Visiting the fatherless can be handled in many different ways. Here are a few suggestions for those of us who are duetting instead of soloing.

- Include the fatherless (or motherless) in your trip with your children to the church picnic, Sunday school, the park, the baseball game, the zoo, the circus, or even to McDonald's.

- Initiate a singles' Sunday-school class or a single-parents' elective for your church.
- Take over an occasional roast, cake, or small gift to the single parent—as you would to a person in bereavement. (Believe me, it's close to being the same thing.)
- Help to lift some of the incredible load of responsibility by asking God for some creative, practical suggestions as to the single parent's needs.
- Don't say, "If there's anything I can do, just call." Call and say, "I have to drive over to such-and-such a place for an hour and a half. Can I take your daughter with me?" Or, go over and say, "I feel like cleaning your bathrooms or your kitchen. *Which* will it be?"

Find the area—financially, emotionally, or, best of all, spiritually—where you can contribute to these bereaved or divorced single parents. Giving your support and your shoulder to lean on is dangerously Christ-like!

Whether you are soloing or duetting at this moment, don't ever listen or take to heart the voices around you that would shout—"God doesn't care about you. Who are you to Him? How can He be involved in the tiny details of your life when He has billions of people to look after?"

We have, carefully preserved, for *all* of us, the marvelous words of Psalm 121. Read these words slowly and inject them into the bloodstream of mind, body and, soul —"He will never let me stumble, slip or fall. For He is always watching, never sleeping. . . . He keeps his eye upon you as you come and go, and always guards you" (Psalms 121:3,4,8 TLB).

Our God never sleeps, and His eyes are always watching and guarding us. Astounding!

I remember when the whole Landorf family took our granddaughter, April Joy, on her first trip to Disneyland. She was just two-and-a-half years old, but the timing was *perfect* for the experience. At one point during the afternoon, she got to meet (and kiss) Minnie and Mickey Mouse. The slides we took of her show unrestrained joy all over her angelic little face. That meeting was the high point of her whole two-and-a-half years. She laughed and enjoyed many things that day, but *nothing* came up to the thrill of touching and talking with Disney's most famous characters. Nothing until the evening parade, that is.

There must have been several thousand people jammed into the Main Street area for the fantastic electric parade of floats that night.

April was in her father's arms so she could see the multitude of tiny, sparkling lights on each float. The number of floats seemed endless, and the music all over the park was simply incredible. All the Disney characters were there, riding these electrical masterpieces. Snow White and her Seven Dwarfs were waving and smiling at the people as they came by . . . Goofy, Donald Duck, Pinocchio . . . and then suddenly there was this enormous float with Mickey and Minnie Mouse sitting way up on top. They were waving to everybody, the music was blaring, balloons were being released, the crowd was cheering and applauding, and in that moment, April took her father's chin in her hand. She looked into his face and, with her blue eyes round with wonder, she said awesomely, "He sees me! Mickey sees me. Minnie sees me! She's waving *at me!* He *sees me!*"

Darling single person, standing in the cheering, waving, applauding crowd and feeling so terribly alone—look up! God never sleeps. He sees you! He sees you!

He really does, and He's not a cartoon, a mythical invention of someone's imaginative mind, but the true-living and real God.

The very same God who, long before the foundations of

the world were laid, chose you.

He sees you—oh, yes—and you are loved! Continue your soloing. Do it in all joy, for He sees you, and He has a plan you can trust!

Recommended Reading

The Long Way Back by Arliss R. Benham, Baker Book House, 1977.

Loving Again by Ginilou DeMarco, Impact Books, 1980.

Celebration of Discipline by Richard J. Foster, Harper and Row, 1978.

Yes by Ann Kiemel, Tyndale House Publishers, 1978.

"Love Is Something You Are," a tape by Ann Kiemel, Word, Inc.

Walking Through the Fire by Laurel Lee, E. P. Dutton, 1978.

Signs of Spring by Laurel Lee, E. P. Dutton, 1980.

Free to Be Single by Elva McAllaster, Christian Herald, 1979.

We Really Do Need Each Other by Reuben Welch, Impact Books.

8
Changepoints . . .

The Holding Pattern

God will not look you over for medals, degrees or diplomas but for scars.

ELBERT HUBBARD

Flying and traveling in jet airplanes all over the world is somewhat less exciting than it appears to be on television commercials. The glamor, comfort, and service recede all too rapidly when you experience five-hour un-scheduled layovers due to bad weather; cancelled flights due to unsold seats; or you get bumped off a plane due to oversold flights.

While flying is still the fastest way to get from point *A* to point *B*, there *is* one facet of traveling by air that I will never instantly accept—at least not without a moment or two of fearful panic.

The cold fear that slides uncomfortably into basic nau-sea happens just as I am airborne or about twenty minutes before landing. I hear the pilot in his best "this-is-merely-routine" voice announce, "Ladies and gentlemen . . . *(a)* we have an unusual amount of air or ground traffic; *(b)* our visibility has just dropped below minimum standards; or *(c)* we have a red light up here showing an equipment malfunction. So, we are going into a holding pattern until we can get a clearance to land."

Then it's white-knuckle and sweaty-palm time.

I think some of you know all about the trauma of a holding pattern, yet you have never even been in an airplane.

Life has presented you this particular changepoint, and the fear and nausea of a holding pattern continually eat away at you. It's a dull, sickening dread, which creeps over you each morning as you experience your first conscious moments. You just want to keep your eyes closed and erase the world, but it's always there.

Your pattern may be holding because of a physical condition. The pain or disease may be steadily deteriorating your body, or it may be the cycling kind, so that just when you think it's gone, it returns again.

For others of you, your holding pattern is the totally unacceptable life-style of a husband, a son, a daughter, or other member of your immediate family.

Perhaps you have a holding pattern that involves an unsolvable circumstance, and you have prayed over it for years. You know God hears those endless prayers of yours, but His answer is not yes or no but, rather, "not now." The frustration of the unanswered *why* continues the holding pattern.

Years of experience in flying have taught me to control my panic when a holding pattern is announced. My hands do not break out in cold sweat, and I'm able to accept the situation far more readily now than earlier in my travels.

As to life's holding patterns, a few years of learning about the character of God have helped me to accept my own personal holding patterns with a little more graciousness and less doubting or questioning. In fact, I have just really learned that . . .

The holding pattern I'm in right now may be the most difficult changepoint of my life, until I stop and realize

Who is holding the pattern!

Let me run that by you again—but in a different way. Here are some examples of holding patterns in the lives of various people I know—including my own. What we all have in common is the *One who holds the pattern.*

This verse in Isaiah was written for those of us in a holding pattern, and it tells us in a beautiful way to look to the *Holder,* not the pattern.

"Though he give you the bread of adversity and the water of affliction, yet he will be with you to teach you— with your own eyes you will see your Teacher" (Isaiah 30:20 TLB).

My friend Linda has very definitely *seen* her Lord and Teacher, but the lessons learned took over a dozen years.

Physical Scars

Linda was happily married, active in Christian work, and delighted with the birth of her first child when an all-shattering and paralyzing pain sent her speeding off in an ambulance to the nearest hospital. Her holding pattern had begun. She was barely twenty-two years old.

X rays revealed she had severe scoliosis of the spine. The disks in her lower back were disintegrating. The pain that had come into her life one afternoon was due to a ruptured disk. Surgery at some point would be her only alternative.

The holding pattern began in earnest. Linda's days consisted of pain and plenty of pain pills. Next came traction, every day. And then a body cast. After that she had lifts in her shoes and injections for pain, and she finally landed back in the hospital.

At this point, her doctor said the inevitable word . . . *surgery* . . . and, "I'm sorry, Linda. I've done all I can, and now I must operate. Someday, when this happens again,

we may not be able to correct the situation, and I sure do
not want that to happen. I don't want you to be paralyzed.
You are so young."

Surgery was scheduled and Linda was unbelievably
frightened. Did she keep this to herself? Did she discuss
it openly with others? I asked Linda about the reactions
of the members of her church. I was interested because
I had just received a letter from a lady who had suffered
from painful arthritis for fifteen years. She had written,
"Because my pain isn't dramatic or visible and is chronic,
the support I receive comes only from my wonderful husband and son—and, of course, my Lord. I learned long ago
that people—even God's—don't want to be around a
problem that has no quick and easy solutions. I have heard
all the pat answers, all the clichés, and more."

Since Linda's back problem was so continual, I wondered how the body of Christ was responding. In Linda's
own words, note carefully what she answered.

"The body of believers I was a part of at this time and
had been a part of for about five years, was not supportive
to me at all. One visitor said to me, 'Linda, you are not
going to go under the knife at your age, are you?' This did
not comfort me in the least. I longed for those who would
help me. I knew God was guiding my life and that I was
in His hand, but how very much I needed to be reassured
of this.

"At this point in my life, all the props had been kicked
out from under me," Linda continued, "and I was standing up only by God's presence in my life and the Scriptures He consistently gave me. No support group was
mine, no assurance of prayer and intercession being made
on my behalf. One woman suggested that if I would clear
the sin out of my life, the Lord would heal me and I would
not have to undergo the surgery at all. I cried out to God
that there please be an other way, not surgery. The

chances of this surgery's being a success were small. My doctor forewarned me that the fusion might not even take, that it happened sometimes.

"I would lie awake at night, not able to sleep because of the pain, and go through the ordeal in my mind, imagining all kinds of things—from what the operating room looked like to what my wheelchair would look like if I would be paralyzed. The day finally came and I was glad. Waiting is hard. And, would you believe? That morning of my surgery, a lady from the congregation called to tell me not to have surgery! Her aunt had just had a spinal fusion and was now permanently paralyzed."

The surgery was completed, and Linda prepared to recover and be well again. She contemplated the two years of pain she had endured since her first abrupt visit to the hospital and decided that she'd learned a lot and had drawn much closer to the Lord, so she concluded that the holding pattern had been worth it.

However, she was not to recover. Months after her surgery, the final X rays showed that the bone fusion had not occurred. The pain and the holding pattern returned. This time with a vengeance.

A second operation was recommended. Linda kept asking the Lord what He was doing and why He was allowing it to happen. Her thoughts were a blaze of fiery questions and concerns. The first surgery had cost one-half the amount of her husband's yearly wages. Fears about finances, who would take care of her little girl, and whether the second surgery would be successful raged within her.

Linda went into the operating room with those fearful terrors inside; however, she also went in with Isaiah 43:-1,2. "Don't be afraid, for I have ransomed you; I have called you by name; you are mine. When you go through deep waters and great trouble, I will be with you. When

you go through rivers of difficulty, you will not drown!
When you walk through the fire of oppression, you will
not be burned up . . ." (TLB). Over and over she repeated
this great promise.

Six weeks after surgery the fusion had taken. The surgery was a medical success, but to her horror, the operation did not take away the pain. It continued! Furthermore, the pain was no longer starting in the morning and
getting stronger by afternoon, but was *on* twenty-four
hours a day.

The pain of the holding pattern was to last like this for
twelve more years. Linda had two more children and
became almost totally crippled. She was unable to do most
of the simple tasks we take so for granted, like loading the
dishwasher or taking the clothes out of the dryer, dusting
the furniture, making a bed, or driving a stick-shift car. To
do anything that caused her to bend was an impossibility.
Of those years, she said, "Most of the ordinary things of
life brought *extraordinary* pain."

Finally, one day in February, Linda's husband took the
reins into his own hands. He took her back to see the
surgeon who had done the second fusion. Linda remembers being angry with her husband's trickery (to get her
there), and she was scared to pieces for fear of what the
doctor would discover. Her worst fears were validated.
The X rays showed that the disks above her lower (fused)
back were now disintegrating. The surgeon carefully explained that a dreadfully serious surgical procedure,
which involved placing a steel rod down her back, was
desperately needed.

It was the lowest point of the holding pattern. Linda
wrote me about her agonizing feelings of that time.

"I knew my back was getting worse, but steel rods had
not been on my agenda for a solution. Neither was the
possibility of wheelchair existence—with three children

to raise, ages fourteen, ten, and six years old.

"In the days to come, the medicine did help relieve my pain some, but enough was there to make me become increasingly frightened. I made a decision. It was a rather irregular decision for me. I was going to go see my new pastor. So far, in my Christian life, I had managed to be able to get it together with the Lord on my own, without pastoral counsel. This time, I would see if he could help. The pain had gotten to me, and I was feeling the most desperate I had ever felt in my life. We had recently changed churches, after nineteen years in one church, and this new church and new pastor seemed to be full of compassion, love, and answers. I made an appointment and went to see him.

"After I got into his office, I felt rather foolish," Linda wrote. "Here sat my pastor across from me, a man of thirty, blond and fair, with piercing blue eyes that never took themselves off of you when you were talking. His deep, warm smile and gentle forceful voice made me feel at ease, however, and I told him my problem. I had known him for about one-and-a-half years now, and had worked with him in the church quite a bit. He had never known that I was in pain. He listened to me so beautifully. I was thinking in the back of my mind, that if he didn't do a thing today to help me, he had heard me better than anyone in fifteen years, and that alone made me feel so valuable.

"We spent about thirty minutes discussing my situation and the pending surgery. At that point, he paused, with his head down (for the first time not looking directly into my eyes) and tears welled up in his eyes as he spoke these words to me: 'Linda, I have never been in pain myself, so I really have a hard time telling you this . . . but, my suggestion to you is that you accept your pain. You have to accept your pain.'

"I became furious. Accept my pain? 'Didn't you hear me, Pastor?' I said. 'I have had it for fifteen years. I have accepted it. That's stupid advice.'

"He went on to gently say that throughout our conversation I had talked of *being* healed and *getting* better, or *having* my pain go away, et cetera. He repeated, 'My advice for you, Linda, is to accept your pain.' I started to cry. He sat opposite me, looking down, leaning forward, his elbows resting on his knees. His hands were folded and he was very solemn. After I gained my composure, I said, 'Well, I have tried everything else, I might as well try this. What do you want me to do to accept this pain?' "

Linda's letter continued, "At this point, he straightened up and looked at me with a warm, gently cocked grin and said just this—he had been waiting for me to will to do what he said—'In the morning, when you have your quiet time, pray like this: Lord, I praise you for this pain. If it is to get better today, I praise you. If it is to get worse today, I'll praise you. And if it is to stay the same today, that's okay, too.' He said I could even tell the Lord I didn't mean it, but my pastor told me to do it.

"I said I would do this and see what would happen. He gave me a quick hug and I left his office."

Linda's letter concluded with, "I had many ambiguous feelings. I felt genuine love from a pastor for the first time in my Christian experience. That was worth something. I thought, *It won't help my back, but it sure helps my heart.* I also felt some anger and disgust that he would suggest I hadn't accepted my pain. I even had flashing thoughts that he was too young and inexperienced in the area of pain to know what he was talking about. But I had told him I would try his plan and so I would. I had absolutely nothing to lose by following his advice."

Early in March, Linda's new church scheduled some

meetings. Pastor Ray Ortlund and his wife, Anne, were to be the main speakers, and the series was geared for the spiritual enrichment of the individual Christian's life as well as the body-life members.

It was an ordinary series of three nights' meetings, but God chose to make it *the* most extraordinary time in Linda's life.

On the last evening, the members in this small church were invited to share whatever they wanted with this body of believers. They would stay as long as the Spirit led. Linda remembers it as being a beautiful time. However, about 8:30 P.M., the Lord seemed to tell her to share about her back and to ask people to support and pray for her upcoming surgery. No one had shared anything about physical needs, so she wasn't about to either. But, by 10 P.M., she could stand it no longer, and for the first time in her church attendance, she presented her needs to an entire congregation. When she finished, someone suggested they pray right then and there, so there was a short prayer, and then the meeting continued for another twenty minutes.

Just as Linda was leaving, as man tapped her on the shoulder and confessed he didn't know what was going on, but asked if he could pray for her. She said yes, and he prayed a very simple and short prayer. By the time she opened her eyes, he was gone.

Linda said of the moment: "I was sort of amused. My thoughts were on how sweet that man was. I chuckled and left the church, picked up the children at my Mom's, and went home. I praised the Lord before going to sleep, for such a good meeting and for helping me be obedient and share with His body of believers. I was lonesome for my husband, who was away on a business trip, and so wished he could have been a part of such a beautiful evening. As

I drifted off to sleep, I chuckled to myself at the thought of the adorable cuddly looking man who had prayed for me."

Then Linda related, "The next morning, as my eyes opened, I felt distressed. My back had gotten so bad, that every morning my husband spent about five to eight minutes getting me into a sitting and then eventually into a standing position. It seemed to take forever, even with his help, to reach the railing in the hall. What would I do this morning? The night before, my daughter had slept with me and helped me up. Last night, she had slept in her own bed. Everyone was asleep and I had to get up.

"I had two hours before the kids had to be at school. I rolled over and began to think of my plan of attack. *Hmm, that didn't cause much discomfort,* so I tried to pull myself up on my elbow and sit for a minute. That was fine, so I pushed myself on up to a sitting position. *No pain so far.* I carefully swung my legs over the side of the bed and put them down on the braided rug beside my bed. *No pain yet. How strange.* I got up and went into the bathroom; still no pain. By this time the children were beginning to awaken, and I got caught up in the preparations of the morning, cooking breakfast and packing lunches.

"I kept it very much to myself," Linda explained, "but it seemed to me that my pain was not there. I was afraid to move. I really thought that the vertebras in my back must be caught somehow in a strange position and were pinching a nerve or something that was causing me to have no pain for the time. I was scared. With my husband out of town, and the kids gone to school, and a mother who does not drive, I anticipated being in a very dangerous predicament.

"As the morning wore on, I was bombarded by an amazing amount of phone calls. It was glorious. People from our church called, offering help of all kinds to me:

prayer, support, helping with my housework, watching the children when I needed them. They cried with me and loved me and I felt so good. This was something totally new to me. I had never, never, ever experienced this at the church we had attended previously. Even though I had had two surgeries and multiple problems, I hadn't received anything like this love and caring before. Around noon, people began dropping by to see me, to hug me, and to pray for me. I felt just marvelous! I realized in the back of my mind that my pain was still not there. Somehow, it worried me, and I longed that it would return and stop playing tricks on me. I was lost without it, I felt uncomfortable and nervous.

"Around two in the afternoon, the pain was still gone. I thought I would call someone whom I could rely on, who would not think I had gone nuts, and tell them. I was anxious for someone else to know my secret. I picked up the phone and called my pastor's wife. I told her what had happened so far, and that I was afraid because my pain of fifteen years was gone. 'What do you think?' I asked her. She said she thought I had been healed when the man from the congregation prayed for me."

Which, of course, is exactly what happened.

God is in charge of *all* healings. In Linda's case, He used a man—a most unlikely man—a man who probably never before, or since, has ever walked up to *anybody* and asked if he could pray for them. It was the end of a fifte-year-old holding pattern.

A miracle, you ask? Yes. And definitely the kind that God ordains. The healing was not dependent on a faith healer, nor did it come through Linda's pastor, or the Ortlunds— although they are very precious people of God. In fact, it didn't have anything to do with Linda's faith or lack of it, or with her spiritual temperature. It had everything to do with God's will for Linda's life, God's sovereignty, and

God's amazing, loving patterns for growing.

When Linda called me and told me about this marvelous God-given experience in her life, I suggested that when she told other Christians about her healing, she keep track of their reactions. Linda is now into the fifth year of her healing, and she has faithfully kept a diary on people's responses, as I once suggested. I never could have predicted the results.

Of course many believers rejoiced with Linda and her family and praised God for His healing mercy. But other reactions, Linda told me, were almost more painful than her back problem.

One woman, who had previously lost her husband, heard Linda's story and wondered aloud, "On what basis does God *choose* to heal?" She kept asking Linda, "On what *merit* were *you* healed?" After all, her husband, a Christian, had died! The woman placed a heavy guilt trip on Linda. Incredible! Here was Linda—feeling *guilty* because she was healed and the woman's husband had died!

On two other occasions, as Linda was sharing her healing, several people got up and left the room. They were unable to handle it. This was very bewildering to Linda.

Once, in a small group, Linda was answering the women's questions about her back when one woman spoke up and asked, "Don't you wish you had shared about your pain with people publicly a long time ago? Then you could have been healed before now." Linda said to me, "It was as if some magic formula had *finally* been put into play and *that* triggered the healing finger of God. I was amazed at such shrunken thinking!"

It was also suggested to Linda that she had to pay God back for doing such a great thing. She was told that she was now under obligation to pray for the man (whom God used in her healing) and for his parents. Later, and with much prayer, she came to the conclusion that her prayers for the man and his parents should never be looked on as payment for her healing.

One person asked to *see* the X rays of Linda's back. It reminded me that the Jews, in Jesus' day, were always asking for a sign that they could *see*. As if *seeing* it made it real and valid.

Still today, Linda is asked by well-meaning and sincere Christians if she feels this healing might be temporary. She says, "I don't feel hurt or offended by this. Most of these people, I feel, have been sincere in asking it. Their motives were not to hurt or make me doubt. My answer to them is that I do not have a clue. They will just have to wait with me and see. I try to project a sort of 'we're in this together as fellow Christians and your guess is as good as mine.' I really try now not to put God in a box in any way. He will do exactly as He wants."

"Still," Linda says, "I have several friends who keep checking with me rather regularly to see if I am still in the holding pattern. I absolutely love, love, love to tell them I've not had a single pain since March 3, 1976!"

When God gives such an obvious healing, we tend to believe that everyone will automatically *see what God has done and then praise Him.* Not so. There can be those unreal reactions from family, friends, doctors and, associates that stun and shock us immeasurably.

Linda's holding pattern of pain has stopped, and God has beautifully interceded in her life. She's a beautiful woman and a treasured friend of mine, but reactions and adjustments continue. Now she's in a new holding pattern, but one *without pain.*

I am praying that Linda will one day use her creative gifts to write out her whole story—particularly the part concerning *after* healing—because we need to learn much more about the lessons of the holding pattern. I've also sensed from Linda that more often than not, the *healee* has to keep turning back to the *Healer* and *Holder* of life's patterns. We need to be reminded of the Healer again and again.

Spiritual Scars

Maybe the changepoint of the holding pattern in your life does not involve a physical problem, but it does concern a husband who doesn't know Jesus as Lord.

Here are some of the things I hear you saying:

1. "How long will the Lord keep me in this holding pattern? I've prayed for my husband ten years, and he's not getting any closer to the Lord."

2. "I buy my husband good Christian books and drag him off to church every chance I get, but he won't have any part of Christianity."

3. "I've tried to be a submissive wife to my husband, but he says he is never going to become a 'Christian' . . . he says it's a disease he doesn't want to get."

4. "Now that *I've* become a Christian, what am I going to tell my husband?"

To the question in statement number one—"How long?"—I have to be up front and honestly say that I don't know. *However,* I will not be guilty of putting God in a box and say, "Wow—with *your* husband I'm not sure God *can* work." We must never limit God, either by methods or by time. It's funny, but I'm always suggesting to the Lord that He save so-and-so's husband by method *A, B,* or *C*— and within six months at the longest, because neither one of these people is getting any younger. Then God does precisely what He planned to do all along. He answers by using the method (or pastor, or accident, or book, or person) of *Q, R,* and *Z!* His timing? That is *never* within our time reference. Some time ago I stopped putting fences and limitations on how I thought God would reach out and touch someone. Even your husband.

To statement number two, let me say, it's not wrong to buy your husband Christian books and to take (*not* drag) him to church; however, it's rarely effective.

I've quoted Jill Renich for years now, and until I find something more profound I'll keep repeating this. She said, "Don't talk to your husband about God. Talk to *God* about your husband."

C. S. Lewis once said that of all the awkward people at your house or at your job, there is only one you can really do anything about. How true.

God doesn't change marriages, he changes individuals. The Lord may have chosen you to *begin* His work. Start walking and living in the center of God's will. Concentrate on that rather than trying to rush or push your husband into a spiritual experience.

As to statement number three, about being a submissive wife to an unsaved man—I'll probably get into hot water over this from some of you, but I'll say it anyway.

The Ephesians letter—the one in which Paul talks about the husband and wife relationship—was first and foremost written to the *Christian* believers, the *men* and *women* of Ephesus. I do not believe we are to be submissive to the non-Christian husband in anywhere *near* the same way we should be to the Christian husband.

In the first place, God wants both men and women to be totally submissive to Him. If a husband is not a Christian, he cannot begin to understand his or his wife's submission *or* commitment to Christ. It's just not possible.

But, for the Christian wife—submission to the Lord has

got to be top priority. Jesus gave up His royal rights to come to earth to serve. To be submissive to God's will. And He was our supreme example. So, for the godly wife, married to an unbeliever—I see her role in marriage as sharing her life as her husband's helpmate, his partner, and his friend. She should do his bidding and be pleasing to him *EXCEPT* when he asks her to violate a Christian principle, a moral standard, or to break one of the express laws of God. Also, if there are children in the marriage, the Christian wife will have to be the spiritual leader in the home. This may not set too well with her non-Christian husband, but it's a necessary principle that must not be neglected.

If being a submissive woman means that you go *against* godly, moral laws and forsake your responsibility for the spiritual training of your children because your husband demands it, then you are not talking about biblical submission as found in Ephesians 5.

It's been a popular concept among some Christian laymen and pastors that a Christian woman must be *submissive at all times* and in all situations, *including* the submission to a non-Christian husband. They have taken this word *submission* and its beautiful meaning and have turned it into something it was never meant to be. The *neglect* and *abuse* these teachings have brought about are appalling. It is no wonder that women all over the world shudder when I even mention the word *submission.* We need to read *all* of Ephesians and see the full meaning of God's word on submission through the Apostle Paul.

Statement number four (what shall I tell my husband) always brings to mind the "show and tell" time our kids had in grammar school. Remember? They would take a new toy, book, even a baby brother or sister to school— show it off, and then tell about it.

When you become a Christian and go home from

church, retreat, or other related activity, it's only natural that you'll be dying to tell *everybody* in the world about your new life in Christ. However, it's probably not *exactly* the right time to tell—rather, it's only "show" time, especially to your non-Christian mate. The "telling" may come later. But, for now, *live* the changed life. Many times I've been told that a woman has left my seminar a brand-new Christian. She's gone home and didn't "tell"—but "showed" the change. Weeks or months later, her husband has said, "You're changed! I like the new you—ever since that day in March (or June, or whenever), you're different. What's happened?" *Then* it's "tell" time, and God has given her a husband with ears willing to hear.

Your God-changed attitudes, responses, and life-style will motivate your husband faster and better than anything you can say!

"Not Now" Scars

I've said publicly, and in private, many times that the hardest answer to prayer has got to be the "not now" answer.

I'm still in a holding pattern with the "not now" answer in regard to my jaw problem. In *The High Cost of Growing* I wrote about the painful syndrome known as Temporomandibular Joint Stress Dysfunction, or TMJ—as it's more commonly known.

Since the publication of that book in 1978, I have continued to pray for healing and to search out new doctors, dentists, physical therapists, diets, and treatments. God has led me to some very special people, and on several occasions, He has really used their skills or techniques to give me some degree of relief from the constant, crushing pain. I am overwhelmed with gratitude for men like Dr. Jack Bamesberger of Pomona, California; Dr. Stephen

Smith of Philadelphia, Pennsylvania; Dr. Richard Ruhe of Garden Grove, California; and especially for Dr. Stephen True of Palm Springs, California. God has used these professionals and many others to help me learn about myself and TMJ, and each of them, in unique ways, has kept me going when I so desperately wanted to quit.

I've now had six years of this holding pattern. I've received thousands of letters about TMJ. They are filled with names of specialists, suggestions as to what might work, personal experiences with pain, and even spiritual judgments as to why I'm *still* in this holding pattern.

I doubt that I will ever know the why of all of this. Honestly, by now—after six years of endurance—I'm not sure the why of it really matters. If I did know or understand the why, would it really change anything? I doubt it.

The place I'm at, in this holding pattern, is hard to explain. I'm not enjoying it. The pain continues to rob me of logic and writing skills; and it distorts my personality so much I know I must be difficult to live with. What's worse, I see no let up.

Just last week a new TMJ "expert" claimed cheerily that her technique would *cure* TMJ in one month's time. I thought: *The prince married the princess, and they lived happily ever after. So much for fairy tales!*

This holding pattern has been helped by professionals who do not promise the moon, but rather say, "Let's try this," then have prayerfully gone to work on my jaw.

I'm also fortunate that, unlike Linda—when the body of Christ in her old church was not supportive—I am surrounded by a beautiful Christian family, friends, and a caring body of church members who, in the bonds of love, continually reach out to me!

Yesterday I received a letter from our precious daughter, Laurie—yes, the same one who kept us on our knees for so long—and here is part of it.

Dear Mom,

I thought all day yesterday, after you left, about your jaw and the dentist you're probably going to see in Newport. I think, for the first time, I felt so little excitement over, "Maybe this one can help Mom." I felt more the feeling, "Don't get excited, just wait and see." I felt sad that my reaction wasn't more supportive, but then again maybe I'm feeling what you're feeling . . . discouragement. I'm beginning to understand that "not now" is a permanent thing. If so—I can't begin to express my sorrow (not pity) I feel in knowing what kind of days lie ahead for you.

I want you to make me a promise. If ever God tells you "why," can I please be the first to know? Because sometimes the anger I feel inside eats at me and causes a distance between my Lord and me until I realize that my feelings are okay, and that I must move out of anger and talk with Him again.

So often lately I'm finding people telling me constantly what your books and your ministry mean to them. How you've touched them, given them hope, encouragement, the will to pick up the pieces and move on. Who does this for you, Mom? Who, what friend, reaches into your heart and says, "I'm here, Joyce, I understand?"

People like me, Dad, Dr. Steve True, your closest friends, can hurt *for* you, and pray—but, oh, the helplessness we feel in helping you through your pain-filled days is so acute!

I say all this, Mom, to let you know that each one of us who loves you does have our own world and lives to live. But, know in your heart, that on those days when your pain is at its worst, we are all here, praying and loving you. Even though we are not there to see that mean enemy of pain in your gentle, hazel eyes—we feel it, and our hearts band together to give you the love and encouragement you need to get through the day.

I guess I answered my own question—it's "us" who help you go on, even though we lack the true understanding of your constant companion (but not friend) . . . pain.

Besides my husband and children, there is a prayer group of a dozen women in Pomona, California, who have held me up for almost all of these six years. My friend Chuck Swindoll has been waiting with me in the "waiting room" for almost four years now. Then there are a few individual women in different parts of the country who have also committed themselves to wait with me, and, on the days when I have no will to go on, the Lord reaches down through them, touches my life, and prods me on.

I dedicated *Mourning Song* to Von Letherer. He is a special man of God who handles all my speaking engagements. He represents singers like Johnny Hall and speakers such as Florence Littauer and Ann Kiemel. I'm privileged and honored to work with him.

Von is not only a man of God but one who suffers daily with constant pain. He is a hemophiliac who bleeds from all his joints. Von's pain battle has taught me much about what exactly God has called us to do.

His beautiful wife, Joann, summed up what this holding pattern is all about, recently, in a letter to me. She wrote:

My Dearest Joyce,

I'm hurting for you tonight, and I feel I must take the time to let you know that you are not alone in your suffering. My heart is heavy and has been so all day.

I share your physical pain deeply! I *do not* understand why—except that you must be loved by the Lord in a special way. I've come to *know first hand* that those who are called to suffer for Christ's glory are a *chosen* few.

"For he [she] is a chosen instrument of mine . . . for I will show him [her] how much he [she] must suffer for my name's sake." Acts 9:15, 16.

This is a verse that the Lord helped me, coincidentally, run into one day when I was hurting so badly for Von.

God spoke so clearly with a loving, gentle voice and said those words. It applies to you, also. What a privilege to be one of the "few chosen instruments" to suffer for the name of Christ. I reminded Von of this last week. Both you and he are special.

My heart is so heavy for you. Perhaps I feel even more defensive than you, but again I do not understand the forever and ever why. I look for the justice, the sense of it, the fairness of it; they *all* have eluded me. I find myself back where I started . . . "For he [she] is a *chosen instrument of* mine."

All of Paul's suffering was relevant; not one shred was wasted. What a godly man, yet so subject to human emotions. And that is what is vital to remember. You are special and chosen, but you are subject to human emotions and feelings. Anger, frustration, rejection, being used, and at times low self-esteem—you know them all. I hurt for the reality of these emotions in your life.

You see, I've learned to allow Von the freedom of feeling all these emotions in response to the intense physical and emotional suffering in his life. I know he is special and chosen, like you, but I don't expect him to be some giant, super star who goes around with a smile painted on his face.

I will allow you to be human in your emotions—I will support you—whatever and *however* you are feeling. Please always remember that.

With love,

JOANN

I wish you had a family like mine, or friends like Joann, but regardless, the truth of their words is valid, and you can draw comfort from them.

If God has not answered yes or no, but instead has given you a "not now" holding pattern—come, take my hand. I'll be with you in your holding pattern. We'll wait together and see just what it is God wants to do with this changepoint. It won't be easy. It probably won't even be fun. But I'd rather be in the center of God's will and in my holding pattern than *any* place in heaven or on earth. Martha Snell Nicholson wrote:

> Oh, Lord of the years that are left to me,
> I give them to Thy hand;
> Take me, and break me, mould me to
> The pattern that Thou hast planned.

This holding pattern is the pattern that *God* has planned. I will rejoice and be glad in it.

We wait together.

Recommended Reading

A Step Further by Joni Eareckson and Steve Estes, Zondervan Publishing House, 1978.

The High Cost of Growing by Joyce Landorf, Thomas Nelson, Inc., 1978; Bantam Books, 1979.

A Woman's Worth by Elaine Stedman, Word, Inc., 1976.

Killing Giants, Pulling Thorns by Charles R. Swindoll, Multnomah Press, 1978.

9
Changepoints . . .

Mothers-in-law,

Empty Nests, and Menopause

God often comforts us not by changing the circum-stances of our lives, but by changing our attitudes toward them.

                                        AUTHOR UNKNOWN

According to my forty-pound dictionary, the word *myth* means, "a traditional story of unknown authorship." An added definition states that a myth tries to explain some phenomenon of nature such as the origin of man or the customs and institutions of life.

Further down the page, I spotted the word *mythomania;* and while it has little or nothing to do with this chapter, I thought you might like to learn a new word and file its definition away in your head in case you should ever be called upon to show your intellectual brilliance. A *mythomaniac,* in psychiatry, refers to a person who has an abnormal tendency to lie or exaggerate. There, wasn't that enlightening? (One more enlightening fact: The plural of *mother-in-law* is *mothers-in-law.*) So, back to myths.

There are literally hundreds of myths or "stories by

unknown authors" about mothers-in-law, and I hardly know where to begin. Here's just a sampling.

1. All mothers-in-law think no one is good enough to marry their child.
2. All mothers-in-law interfere with their adult children's decisions.
3. All mothers-in-law nag, whine, and complain that their adult children do not write, visit, or call enough.
4. All mothers-in-law instruct and inform their daughters-in-law on the basics of housekeeping, cooking, grooming, and raising children.
5. All mothers-in-law regard their sons-in-law in the same manner. Hoping—that given seven days, like a cold —they'll go away.

The key problem with these five statements is the word *all.* Lumping *all* mothers-in-law together is like saying all flowers are alike. However, many mothers-in-law do have one (or several) of these traits, so the myths about the in-law life continue and flourish. Incidentally, I'm not suffering from a touch of mythomania about mothers-in-law! My information comes from all over the country, and out of many mouths.

The world around us has shoved mothers-in-law into its own mold. It depicts us as warped, insensitive, and totally unbecoming women. We are the butt of jokes. The image that clings to us is much like that of Disney's wicked stepmother, and it's almost impossible to shake it off. We have become distorted caricatures of what we are supposed to be.

Let me pause, right here, and ask you. What kind of a mother-in-law are you? Are the five myths I shared not myths at all but realities in your relationship with in-law children? I hope not. But I talk to thousands of women, get a considerable amount of mail, and there seems, even in the *Christian* world, to be a large discrepancy between what we *should* be and what we *are*.

One woman wrote and asked me to talk about, or write something positive and good about, the role of mothers -in-law. She told of hearing a minister give the keynote address at a large denominational conference. Twice the man referred to his mother-in-law. First, he described something as being "colder than a mother-in-law's kiss." Later, he tossed off, "Oh, well, you have to take the seed to get the tomato."

The woman's letter ended with, "Is it any wonder that young couples have in-law problems? They have been brainwashed and not only by the world, but by Christians as well, to believe the worst about us. I believe there is a real need to change the status of a mother-in-law."

I agree. But I don't know what to do with other mothers -in-law. I only have me to work on. In our defense, I will say that for every "bad" mother-in-law I've heard about, I've heard of or met many others who were superior examples! They are beautiful, caring Christian mothers-in-law. I personally have had one mother-in-law and two stepmothers-in-law, and all of them have been marvelous!

How do you change the status of a mother-in-law? How do you keep from falling into the same trap and patterns? I'll get to those of you who are already in the mother-in-law changepoint a few pages down the way. But, for the rest of you young women, here are some guidelines.

Preventative Medicine—Praying

Actually, I became a "mother-in-law" *before* my children were married. It dawned on me one day when my kids were thirteen and fifteen, that while I'd never give birth again, the day would come when I'd have two more children. A daughter- and son-in-law—if marriage was in God's plans for Rick and Laurie.

I figured the Lord wanted me to get a head start in learning the gentle graces of being a mother-in-law.

At first I didn't know how one began "in-law-ing," but surely since mothers-in-law had such bad reputations, there must be more at stake here than merely sitting in the second pew on the wedding day and smiling at everyone.

I began with my prayer life. Each day I prayed about the two young people, wherever they were in the world, and whoever they were. I attacked the problem defensively. I prayed that God would begin a bonding of love in me for these two unknown in-law children. I prayed for them and their families, for their spiritual life, their education, and the lessons of growing that would come to them. The last part of my prayer always centered on that moment in the future when my child would say, "Mom, this is the one I'm going to marry." I prayed that I would be able to accept my *child's* choice.

Brave prayers? Yes. A little naive? Perhaps. But, I refused to box God in and limit Him to the world's specifications and standards. Also, I honestly believed and took Him at His Word . . . that He hears and answers our prayers.

What happened was truly remarkable. I began taking my first steps toward really trusting God's plan and to loving two unknown, invisible people.

A few years later, I met my first in-law child—Teresa Pursell. I experienced the pleasant shock and delight at meeting someone I'd prayed for but had never seen. I wrote in detail about this refreshing encounter in *Mix Butter With Love*. And, now, seven years and two beautiful grandchildren later, I can still say, "I *love* being that girl's mother-in-law!'"

I can hear you say, "That's fine about Teresa being the right one and the special person you prayed for—but what if Rick had brought home Miss Wrong; or worse, just went off and made some person his live-in roommate?"

Good question, that one. As it turned out, that's exactly what I began asking myself in regard to our daughter.

My husband and I were looking forward to the time when both our children would be grown and be out on their own. We knew, so long ago, that they would make very *special* adults. We had lovingly trained them in God's ways. We had tried to discipline them without breaking their spirits, and we felt we had held them with open arms. We were *ready* to release them, and in many ways I believe we did succeed. However, the Lord had some extraordinary concepts to teach us about releasing. He used Laurie as a blackboard to write out our lessons.

Laurie started dating at sixteen, as was the plan at our house, and some of those boys, and experiences she had, raised many serious doubts and questions in my mind. I had second thoughts on the validity of my advance prayer life for in-law kids. I wondered, when she brought home her "this is him" person, if I would feel the marvelous "clunk" inside me (like a piece of my heart dropping into its exact place), as I had felt with Teresa.

It was when she was eighteen that Laurie began to regularly date a Christian young man from our church. Almost from the first, they seemed fairly serious about their relationship, and Laurie was radiant with the unmistakable glow of love.

As she went into the second year of a four-year relationship, both Dick and I began having some solemn apprehensions and misgivings. Our daughter began a frightening metamorphosis. It was not the usual kind. For one thing, the glow that had lit her face so ethereally, flickered and then went out. Instead of their love for each other transforming them into a loving couple—as it so often does when everything is so right—the love between them changed and slowly soured in their hearts and on their faces.

Laurie, our high-spirited girl, our enthusiastic-for-life girl, lost her spontaneous gaiety. She lost her well-developed sense of humor, and suddenly we could no longer tease her as we had freely done as a family, nor could she dish it out and tease us back.

She seemed to trade her own ebullient personality in for a bland I-couldn't-care-less attitude toward all of life. It truly frightened me, and because I was the first to really see the changes, I was alone with my jarring observations for quite some time. Eventually, Dick and the rest of the family saw the changes in Laurie, and then we all wondered about the hows, whys and wherefores of the situation. We had the feeling that we'd all had the same bad dream about her only to find that we were wide awake and what was happening was no dream, but reality.

Once I asked Laurie how she was doing with the Lord, and her defiant answer, *"I'm just fine, Mom!"* interrupted my heartbeats. I knew *we* were in trouble. Not just Laurie, but all of us—as a family. We were either to be shattered by this ordeal or to be reconciled, and God would have to be the one to do the miraculous to mend us all.

Everything I knew about Christianity, psychology, and the rigors of marriage said this particular relationship of Laurie's would not work. I hasten to add here that at no time did I feel that my Laurie was "too good" for this young man. It was simply a case of *both* of them being very wrong for each other. They tore each other apart, and day after day, the wounds deepened.

Laurie's physical health began a rapid deterioration, and while she broke up with the young man several times, she always went back. It was now a painful romance. I upped my timetable on nagging. I cried, pleaded, begged, stomped my feet, humored her, and sent her to friends for counseling. Basically, I jumped all over both of them. I urged them to see that the arguments and sharp disagreements they had now with families, friends, and between themselves would only *increase* with marriage.

Three wedding dates were made and broken, and as Laurie went into the fourth year of this tragic affair, I grew weary with desperation.

This wasn't how it was supposed to be. Hadn't I prayed for my children *and* in-law children? Why couldn't I simply accept this young man as Laurie's husband? Since I saw the brokenness of their lives, I had tried to advise, counsel, and steer them out of harm's way—but it was all so futile.

Maybe the changepoint you are in right now is where I was for those agonizing four years. Your son or daughter's life-style and/or relationship with others is utterly foreign to you. Their once strong beliefs in Christ seem to have been blown away by the winds of change. You get no real rest at night, and daily you long to see the unbroken circle of hands around your table. Take heart from these next words:

Never, in the whole four years, did I ever see God working in Laurie's or her friend's life; neither did I ever feel God's peace, nor was I comforted.

All of that was very confusing to a believer like me. Confusing, mainly because we live in a world that constantly tells us to trust our decisions to what we see happening and what we feel inside. "If it feels good—do it." Desperately, as Christian parents, we want more than ever to *see* and feel God at work! When we don't see and feel Him, it's as if somebody pushed us out of an airplane at ten thousand feet and we've never had jumping lessons or packed our parachutes.

Some of us have been devastated by the words of another Christian mother, who says of her prodigal son or daughter: "All the time, I didn't know where he/she was, but God gave me a complete peace about it." We think, *That's wonderful for you, but why didn't He do that for me?*

It's important to believe God—not in what He does or does not do, and certainly not in how He operates, but in *who* He is. Right now these circumstances involving your children need—no, *demand*—our unflinching, undying obedient trust to the sovereignty of God.

Having children is a little like building ships. There comes a day when you have completed everything, and the ship needs to be launched. You christen it and send it sliding down to the sea of life. You trust it will not only float but sail! With your children, it's now up to God, and you trust Him even though you know all about the storms that may overtake them.

I can honestly say I had that kind of blind trust in the Lord, but after four years of Laurie's continually deteriorating relationship, we were all desperate for a healing. I did what Sarah, Rachel, and many others did in the Old and New Testaments . . . I took matters into my own hands and ran ahead of the Lord.

In November of that fourth year, I told the Lord that Thanksgiving would be the day we would all talk to Laurie. We, as her immediate family, would tell her she had to break off this devastating relationship. We would not stand by and watch her go over a cliff and destroy herself any longer. I asked the Lord for the right words. Instead of giving me the appropriate remarks, He commanded sternly, *"Be quiet."*

I told Him I didn't think He knew how long this had gone on or how serious the whole thing had become, and asked again what He wanted me to say. Once more, the Lord said, "I want you to be quiet."

Now, I wish that I could say I've never disobeyed the Lord, especially when He was so concise; however, on Thanksgiving day I was *not* quiet. I deliberately disobeyed the Lord. After the turkey and the pumpkin, Rick, Teresa, Dick, and I eloquently went down mental checklists and told Laurie that if she didn't break off her engagement, she would go over the cliff and nobody could save her.

When I gave my great, logical summation at the end of the other speeches, Laurie got up and with, "That's enough, Mom!" walked right out of our lives. It was as if the dying was over—we could shut the coffin lid and bury her. She was gone.

Clearly I heard the Lord say, "I *told* you to be quiet."

Let there be no misunderstanding here. There is a time (and you'll hear the Lord, as to when) for sitting down with our almost-adult child and saying, "Your behavior— life-style—sinning—whatever—is not acceptable. We could not live like that. As your parents we have to tell you —we hate the life you're living and can see no future in it; but, *you*— you we love. You, we care for, and you we will pray for until they put a lily in our hand and close the lid!"

It is right for us to state our beliefs—to speak up when our children are souring in life; and it is also right to state our love, and to give our supportive approval to this child who so desperately needs it.

But there is also a time, after all's been said, to be quiet.

I really blew it that Thanksgiving day. I had asked the Lord for wisdom. He gave it. I refused it!

In early December I was flying to Omaha, Nebraska, for a seminar on the family, and with a very heavy heart I confessed my disobedience to the Lord. I asked Him what I should do now. I'll never forget what happened next. I was warmly forgiven, and then the Lord gave me the idea of writing Laurie a letter. I should say I loved her, but I should release her to go "over the cliff" if she wanted to. I should free her to do whatever she, at twenty-two years of age, wanted to do. I always felt I *had* released her; but, after I deliberately disobeyed God, it was apparent I was still holding on. I wrote the letter.

When I returned home, Dick was away on a business trip. There was a letter on the kitchen table, and a note clipped to it read:

> Dearest Mrs. Dorf,
> I've written this letter to Laurie. Read it,
> and if you agree, please mail it to her.
> Love,
> MR. DORF

I read his letter. It contained almost word for word what mine did. I called Laurie and asked if I could send them to her. "Yeah," she mumbled and hung up.

Both Dick and I knew what we had written was of the Lord, but neither of us were prepared for what happened. Laurie received the letters and misread each line of them.

She called the young man and told him that we had written her. She said we no longer loved her and that we had told her to go to hell, so why didn't they go to Las Vegas and get married? He agreed.

Before they left town, Laurie decided to stop at the house of one of her few remaining friends. Gayle is a

Christian and, as I wrote in a previous chapter, we had prayed for years that one Christian peer person would hold our child's head above the water. When Laurie told her friend where they were going, Gayle reminded Laurie that she had always wanted a big wedding, a white dress, and her mom singing "Sunrise, Sunset" as she walked down the aisle. In a matter of minutes, Gayle had talked Laurie out of going. (It was such a simple suggestion—I would never have used that tack!) They didn't make it to Las Vegas; but, they didn't stop seeing each other, either.

Christmas came and went, and the whole day can be summed up in Dick's exhausted comment as we finally crawled into bed that night. "Is it because I'm getting older, or has Christmas *always* been such a drag?" he said. We had gained a daughter-in-law, but we had lost a daughter along the way.

In January, a young man named Terry Jacob phoned Laurie. He had met Laurie at Mount San Antonio College when she was eighteen and a freshman there. When they were introduced, someone told Laurie that Terry's girl friend had just been killed in a bike accident. After asking him a few questions, Laurie said, "You need my mom's book." Then she gave him the book and promised to be his friend if he ever needed to talk about the death of his girl.

I don't know if it was love at first sight with Terry, or not, but soon he was calling Laurie for dates. She had just begun her relationship with the other young man, so she was willing to talk to Terry about death and dying, but she didn't want a romantic relationship. Laurie was relieved when he went off to Arizona State University in Tempe, Arizona. But Terry would call her in the summer, anyway. She'd say no to dates, and that's the way it went for the next few years.

While Terry was at Arizona State, he was spotted by the scouts for the Saint Louis Cardinals baseball team, and was signed up to pitch for their farm club.

When he called Laurie that January day, it was just before he was to go back to Florida for spring training. He didn't ask her for a date—in fact, it was only at the maneuvering of a friend that Terry phoned her at all—but, instead, he asked her how her parents were. "We're estranged—not talking or anything," she admitted. There was a long pause and then Terry asked, "Is it because of your relationship with so-and-so?" When she said it was, Terry launched into a speech that must have been very painful for her. He told her that no one person should come between the relationship she had with her parents or her family. That her parents and brother were great, and nothing or nobody should separate her from them! (I *love* this boy!)

In order to stop him, Laurie invited him to come to dinner the next night to, as she put it, "Meet my roommate, Kim. You'll just love her!"

Terry accepted, came to dinner, met Kim—but fell deeply in love with Laurie. And the rest of the story reads like a highly romantic novel by England's Barbara Cartland!

In February, I met Terry, and I'll never forget it. Dick opened the front door. Laurie and Terry came bubbling into our entrance hall. I came down the stairs, turned, and just stared at Terry. It took every ounce of control within me not to make a flying leap over the staircase railing, hug him breathless, and shout, "So *you're the one* I've been praying for since she's been thirteen!" (I practiced self-control, waited two days, and *then* I told him. I also promised that if Laurie didn't marry him, I would.)

The following September, Laurie, dressed in an exquisite ivory lace and chiffon gown, walked down the aisle on her father's arm; I sang "Sunrise, Sunset," my husband gave the bride away and gave them both our blessing. They were married, and it was right.

Terry had become a Christian after he read *Mourning Song.* He had gone back to his girl's church, and several months after her death, he had accepted Christ. He told Laurie that a baseball coach had gotten him started, with several other players, in weekly Bible study and prayer meetings. God was preparing Terry all the time. He said his one prayer for the past three years had been, "Lord, give me Laurie Landorf as my wife."

When I asked their permission to tell and to write their story, both Laurie and Terry eagerly said yes. But the first time they heard me talk about it, I was speaking for chapel at Azusa Pacific College. Afterward I asked Terry if he wanted to withdraw his permission or change his mind. He smiled and told me he wanted me to tell it, but that I just didn't tell it right.

"What's wrong?" I asked.

"Well," he explained, "there I was, pitching ball for the Cardinals. And, with each pitch, I'd say, 'Lord, give me Laurie Landorf as my wife.' Each time God would answer back, 'Not now!' I never thought the Lord was working, and I never thought I'd ever marry Laurie."

Here we are—right back to our frantic "need" to see God working and to feel His peace or presence. Yet, without either of those tangible aspects, God was working in Laurie's life, Terry's life, the other young man's life, and certainly in our family's life.

He is a sovereign God, and has made plans for us even while we were being formed. Read Psalms 139:16, for it says, "You saw me before I was born and scheduled each day of my life before I began to breathe. Every day was recorded in your Book!" (TLB).

Now, for those of you who did not, for one reason or another, ever have the added advantage of early preventative-medicine-praying, here are some suggestions for this changepoint called "mother-in-law," that you now face.

1. Accept your in-law child as is. Remember how, before you were married, you thought you could correct all the bad habits and erase all the flaws your husband-to-be had? Then, you found the only person you could ever do much about was not him—but yourself. So it is with in-law children. If he or she needs changing, ask God to do it; because then, *when* change comes, it will be from within and done by God. That's the best kind.

2. Be an emotional and a spiritual support. Do nothing and say nothing that would say you were unloving, unloyal, or unsupportive. There are enough people in the world who won't approve of us, who will reject us, even taunt and humiliate us. We all need a safe place to recover from the battle wounds. Make your house and your heart that safe place for your in-law children as well as your own son and daughter.

Continue daily to pray for this in-law child. It's never too late to start, but watch out—God does delightful things, and you may be surprised.

3. Maintain a "realness" policy. Now that you have a son- or daughter-in-law, they will see you as your family sees you. Unvarnished, unguarded, possibly even unwashed or unbrushed. Real love requires real people to be themselves. To try to be something you are not, to put on airs or take on some pseudopersonality will not stand the test of time. Kids can spot phonies, so if you really want to change the image of a mother-in-law, you'll have to work at it. It's just not accidentally achieved.

Before I leave mothers-in-law, I can hear you ask, "Yes, but what if your child chooses the wrong partner? Or, the partner's personality changes, or the partner is into abuse or extramarital affairs? What then? What if they go over the cliff?"

These are penetrating concerns and hurts, and the real heartache of everyday life is that these things do happen — but when our children make *their own* decision to marry—it is exactly that. Their decision. Not yours, or mine. So, then, we have to be sure about our *response* to them.

There's a time to affirm our love for them, and a time to tell them gently how we feel about their life-style, actions, sinning—whatever. Wait for the Lord's timing on this last one!

Jesus hated sin, but loved the people. That's our best rule-of-thumb advice on this subject of prodigal children (our own, or our in-law). We need to reaffirm our love to the person but at the same time to be honest about the situation.

I may not know you personally, but I do know God, and He can give you a gracious spirit. He can make you a wise and gentle mother-in-law, in even the *worst* of circumstances . . . He can even do *miracles* with the most stubborn of us all.

The Empty Nest

Incredibly, about the time in our lives we become mothers-in-law, several new alarming changepoints set in.

Our children begin leaving our secure little nest just as we seem to be getting the hang of it all, and we realize things are getting very quiet. No one seems to need a clean shirt or a sack lunch quite the way they used to.

Our husband is reaching the height of his career, position, or talents, and he's spending more time away from the nest. We suspect he's going through some kind of a mid-life crisis, but we don't know for sure. What we do know is that, from the peculiar rumblings within our body, menopause can't be far away.

Another important consideration when speaking about empty nests is the issue of priorities. If a woman *rigidly restricts* herself, her mind, her creative talents, and her sole attention to children—placing their needs and wants above her husband's, or even her own desires—she is in for a *dreadful* time during the season of empty nests.

The biblical concept of marriage and the family is just that. Marriage first. Family second. There must be *strong* steellike ties between husband and wife if there is ever going to be any strength and endurance to the family.

When we rearrange this two-point priority list, we are in for some grievous heartaches. Our sadness becomes inevitable.

Consider this: For years we have been in a busy frenzy, what with taking care of husband, babies, and house. We have gone back to school or taken an outside-the-home job, and have involved ourselves in a thousand different home, community, and church projects.

Now, even before we realize it, our children have been steadily leaving; old what's-his-name is more like an established habit than a husband, and our personalities and lives are about as vivacious and useful as a yo-yo without a string.

It is no wonder, then, that so many of us dread the changepoints of time.

The Menopausal Event

Almost overnight, as it were, we are burdened with depressing thoughts, empty houses, maddening hot flashes, shocking personality changes, and an increasing irritability—physical and emotional—while in the act of making love. Then, because women who whine and complain bore us silly, and we don't want to be like them, we suffer and wonder in a sad silence.

Adding to our dread are whispered old wives' tales and myths—perpetuated by mothers, friends, and even the medical profession.

Just What Is It?

Pure and simply, menopause is the cessation of our menstrual flow. After twelve consecutive months of no monthly period, we are menopausal. You may hear the word *climacteric*— but, not to worry, it's just a broader term used to describe the whole process.

Symptoms of menopause tend to begin gradually, in most cases, when we are between forty and fifty years old. Once in a while, it's not a gradual turning off, but an abrupt one; and, in some cases, it can happen while we are in our mid-twenties.

It's a very busy time for our bodies. The shutting down procedure is happening. Not only do we not have a period, but even the ovaries close shop. They don't make eggs anymore, and there is a progressive decrease in the production of ovarian hormones.

The symptoms of menopause can bring real (not imagined) physical and emotional discomfort, even pain. The problem is caused by the fact that although the adrenal glands continue to produce some estrogen, it is not enough. So we are deprived of a very important hormone.

Good Housekeeping Woman's Medical Guide states that this hormone is the one that "stimulates breast development, determines the quality of voice, keeps skin smooth and free of coarse hair." Offhand, I'd say the level of this hormone is a big factor in our overall sense of well-being.

Two of the most common problems with the changepoint of menopause are the infamous hot flashes, and a condition known as vaginal atrophy, which is caused by the drying and shrinking of vaginal tissue.

What Can We Do?

There are a number of things we can do as we begin to experience menopause. I hope, if you are discouraged because of this particular changepoint, or you're confused by all the statements *and* myths you've heard, that this chapter will give you new insights, hope, and practical help.

Look at some common myths about menopause—and, remember, some women believe them.

1. Hot flashes are normal and there is *nothing* you can do about them.

2. Everything about menopause is absolutely dreadful!

3. Because of vaginal pain, your sex life is over with the onset of menopause.

First of all, the medical profession estimates that about 10 percent of all menopausal women do not experience hot flashes; yet another 10 percent have them continually. The rest have them occasionally. There is a *physical basis* for hot flashes, but before this was established, women suffering from them were thought to be hysterical or even mad, depending on the severity of their symptoms.

The *Los Angeles Times* carries a weekly medical advice question and answer column, authored by a medical doctor. Last week the headline read, "Coping with Hot Flashes," so I read it.

A woman wrote, saying she thought she was having hot flashes, and she asked the doctor to explain why it was happening and to tell her if anything could be done.

The good doctor did an excellent job of describing the effect of decreased estrogen in the nervous system, but not before he made me angry.

He brushed the whole problem off his neat little clipboard by saying that hot flashes may be embarrassing, but they are not dangerous. That may be true. But, talk to any woman who has suffered recurring attacks, and she'll say they are not nearly so embarrassing as they are downright painful.

Then the doctor really endeared himself to me when he naively suggested, at the end of his answer, that if you were having hot flashes, you should merely choose a dress with a lower neckline and wear cotton clothing—"to help the heat escape."

Good grief! I may be dumb, but I'm not stupid. I needed a second opinion. I've read books, talked to women (both pre- and post-menopausal), but it wasn't enough. So, I called my friend Mary Jean (an RN) and asked her to set up a phone appointment with her doctor and my friend, Dr. Jitendra Bhatt. He is a medical doctor with a speciality in gynecology, obstetrics, and infertility, and he is a fellow of the American College of Obstetrics and Gynecology. Those are impressive credentials, but what really makes him special to me is that he is Laurie and Teresa's doctor. Last July, Dr. Bhatt "brought" me Richard, and, in September, James—my two beautiful grandsons!

"Dr. Bhatt, may I talk to you about the myths and

strikeouts of menopause?" I asked.

"Sure!" he answered, and we were off. Here are some of the topics we covered.

Hot Flashes and Vaginal Atrophy

Dr. Bhatt, along with many other gynecologists, does *not* believe there is *nothing* you can do about the physical discomfort of hot flashes.

Since it's an estrogen deficiency that upsets the whole hormonal balance (making the body's heat-regulation system go on the blink, too), low dosages of estrogen have been the primary choice of treatment.

Some doctors feel this is a controversial choice, and there are disagreements about the safety of estrogen replacement.

Dr. Bhatt quickly pointed out that there are some patients who cannot, and must not, take estrogen. They may have cancer, heart problems, or some other condition that will not allow their bodies to tolerate estrogen. But even then, there are synthetic substitute drugs which, when given, will ease (if not take away) the hot-flash discomfort and other menopausal symptoms.

For most of us, if the smallest dosage of estrogen is given from the first to the twenty-fifth of the month, and then, from the twenty-first to the twenty-fifth, a progesterone hormone is added, the combination *relieves* and *removes* the most upsetting symptoms associated with menopause.

There are many estrogen products—pills, injections, and creams—and they are all designed for long-term therapy. By the way, there are even estrogen creams that can be applied to the vaginal tissues. The cream helps to restore and lubricate the tissues, thereby eliminating the pain felt during sexual intercourse.

Basically, what Dr. Bhatt conveyed to me was that women do not have to dread the coming of menopause. There is help. More specifically, he made it clear that we *don't* have to "learn to live with the problems" or "suffer through it" for years.

Who Can We Go To?

It's funny, but —if we want to—we'll spend hours figuring out where we will get a good deal or a real bargain on groceries, clothing, cars, or real estate. In short, we shop around. Yet, when it comes to finding the right doctor or specialist, we are somehow so intimidated by the medical profession, we take whomever we can get.

Doctors are not gods. Medically, they *are* highly trained human beings. We have sometimes deified them to the point that we believe they cannot make mistakes. Yet, in truth, *all* of *us* are all too routinely capable of errors.

A doctor's medical qualifications, credentials, and peer-group reputation are *very* important! But I have to add two more factors: The doctor for us must be able to listen and at least give the impression that he cares.

I wish every pregnant woman I know could go to Dr. Bhatt to have her baby. He is a beautiful person and skilled in the healing arts. I wish all of us who are about to enter menopause—or are in it already—could go to him as a gynecologist. But that's not possible.

So, how do we find a doctor who treats a woman and her body with respect? How do we know if he listens or cares? I asked Dr. Bhatt, and here's what he suggested:

1. Ask your friends about their experiences with their doctors. Go to a doctor who's been recommended. Call and make an appointment.

2. On your first visit, whether it's a physical examination

or a consultation, try to determine if the doctor is listening to you and whether he seems to care.

I personally would suggest you ask what would appear to be a rather dumb question, and see how the doctor handles it. Does he laugh, shake his head, and evade the question? Does he say, as one doctor said to me, "That's the most stupid question anyone's ever asked me," and walk out of the room? Does he brush aside your question? Or, does he understand that the question, asked by someone without his medical expertise, is justified and valid? Does he give you an explanation, or supply you with printed instructions, have his nurse talk to you about specifics, and in general, answer your question? If so, then that's the doctor you're looking for.

Dr. Bhatt suggests that when you find this doctor, especially when menopause is on your changepoints' horizon, ask for your next appointment to be the doctor's last one in the day. That way you can talk without interruptions about your concerns. Doctors' schedules, as you know, are usually jam-packed and running behind, so it's unfair to expect them to be patient and listen to your long list of questions. Then, tell the doctor you want to bring your husband with you. If your gynecologist does not think your husband needs to be with you for the consultation—believe me—this is *not* the doctor for you.

Dr. Bhatt stated very clearly that if a husband participates in the consultation, at least one-half of the job of understanding is done. This illuminating time of communicating between husband, wife, and doctor not only lets your husband become aware of the problems you're facing, but gives him a greater understanding of what's happening, and it also gives him a greater ability in handling this frustrating time.

One young woman who experienced an early menopause, told me her husband never *did* understand. She said much could have been accomplished if her husband could have heard the doctor's opinion and been free to ask his own questions. Incidentally, this same young woman told me that after two years of great discomfort, personality changes, and vaginal pain, she had changed doctors and was now on low dosages of estrogen. "Is it working?" I asked. Her answer? She almost shouted, "It's turned my whole life around!"

Your choice of doctors, or the decision to go with estrogen therapy, are certainly personal matters and up to you, but I hope this chapter has set your heart and mind to considering what thousands of women are finding by trial and error: We must have a doctor who keeps up with the rapidly advancing world of medicine, and we must know he respects us and makes our fears and problems his concerns.

For years I have read the Scripture about our bodies being the temple of the Holy Spirit. I've generally only thought of that verse in conjunction with what we've put *into* our bodies. "Don't smoke, drink, or take drugs, and so forth." The point is well taken, but after my conversation with Dr. Bhatt, and after hearing the late Dr. David Hernandez speak so highly of gynecology and the intricate and special way God has created women—I wonder if we missed an important message. Here's the verse in its entirety. "Do you not know that your body is a temple of the Holy Spirit within you, which you have from God? You are not your own; you were bought with a price. So glorify God in your body." (1 Corinthians 6:19, 20 rsv).

Being careful and selective about what we put *into* our bodies is important, but so is how we use our bodies, how we treat or abuse our bodies, and how well we respect our bodies. After all, God is now within this earthly body of mine, and to glorify God *in my body* I had better get a clear picture of what I'm dealing with.

Maybe you've looked in the mirror lately and decided you didn't have a whole lot going for you in the body department. Don't worry about it. I'm not talking about the shape you are in, or are not in. I *am* asking you to look on your body as a *temple* for the Lord, and then give that body the *respect* it deserves.

There is no reason for you to dread these changepoints of mothers-in-law, empty nests, and menopause in your life. There is no reason, either, for you to be miserable and add extra trauma to the people close to you. I urge you to put your trust in the Lord and when the time is right, seek the best professional help.

Let me go back to Psalm 139. Remember? It says that even before I was born—while I was being formed in the seclusion of my mother's womb—God planned out all my days. These words were written for *all* of us. God has planned our days—even these days—and our bodies are the temples in which He lives.

Take care of that temple!

Recommended Reading

What Wives Wish Their Husbands Knew About Women by James Dobson, Tyndale House Publishers, 1977.

Mix Butter with Love by Joyce Landorf, Harvest House, 1974.

Choices: Realistic Alternatives in Cancer Treatment by Marion Morra and Eve Potts, Avon Books, 1980.

Good Housekeeping Woman's Medical Guide by David Rorvik, Avon Books, 1976.

10
Changepoints...

The Beauty of Winter

It is the winter of my life.
I see the snow sparkling outside in the twilight
Yet I am not cold or alone.
I am warmed by the fires of my memories
And all the women of God who have lived,
loved, and then opened their hands and let go
Are here with me.

Is this changepoint time the winter season of your life? Are you waking up in the morning wondering where the years and the people have gone? Remember on your birthday once, someone asked you how it felt to be sweet sixteen and you shrugged your shoulders? Birthdays haven't made the difference. It was the gradual intake of experiences and the progression of the years that has shaped you, your thought processes, and your feelings. You were too active and too involved with life to notice the changing seasons, but autumn is over and winter has come.

"Shh," you say. "Don't talk of growing old. I want to ignore it for as long us possible." You are not alone in your feelings. In all the mail I've received in the past twelve years regarding the books I've written, I've had hundreds of suggestions as to what my readers want me to write about. None have asked for the subject of aging. Yet, winter comes to all of us.

"But I don't want to read about it, face it, or look back and be reminded of past failures. Especially, if I've not too many days of future left." I understand and hear clearly what you are saying. But we *are* growing older each moment.

Most of us are fearful of the winter winds of declining health and dwindling finances. We are saddened by the snows that silently fall over the graves of our loved ones. And since the dark comes quickly in the winter, we are frightened of being alone.

Perhaps this chapter will encourage you to find the beauty in the wintertime of your life. I pray so!

I'm always amused at our reticence to talk about our ages. Many times, after I've spoken of the different segments of the changepoints in our lives, I'll ask several hundred women before me, "Now, how many of you are growing old?" Only a very few women in the audience will raise their hands.

Isn't that odd? Even little four-year-old girls are growing old. But none of us seem willing to admit it. We have been strangely convinced by all the media, Madison Avenue, TV commercials, and many other voices around us that growing old is completely unacceptable in our society. We cannot have dry skin or horrid age spots. We have to stay forever young and forever beautiful!

When I mention my age in a seminar (I'm forty-nine at this writing.), there is always a gasp of surprise that runs through my audience. I'm sure it's not because they are thinking how much older or younger I look, or whatever, but because they are stunned that I would publicly reveal my age—at all!

Stamped across our ages are the words *TOP SECRET.* Why is that? I feel certain our determination to avoid the aging process and our reluctance to reveal our exact age is due, in part, to this: We have had advance programming all our lives, which has put the aging process in the very worst light!

You might have had a mother, or grandmothers, aunts, or cousins by the dozens who made growing old a cardinal sin. Then, when *they* reached that changepoint, they affirmed it, and made every horrible thing they said come true. You shuddered and decided all winters were filled with dark, depressing days, which finally ended by being swallowed up in death.

Another problem with growing old is the lifelong habit of caring very much what others think of us and the problem of forever comparing ourselves with others. Heaven help us, if we do not grow old as gracefully or as wonderously as Mrs. Continually Perfect or Mrs. Absolutely Spiritual.

It seems to me that my mother never got trapped in the aging battle—nor did my Grandmother Uzon. Both women took life as it came. One day at a time. If they heard the ugly rumors about the difficult winters to come, they never complained or gossiped about them. They seemed to always live in the productive springtime of their lives, yet they harvested fruit right up until they died. They were like the orange trees that blossom and bear fruit, unbelievably, at exactly the same time.

Both my mother and grandmother did their very best with what talents, skills, and years they had been given.

My mother's time here was very brief. She died at the age of fifty-seven, but anyone who knew her remembers her as a woman who used up each moment as if it were her very last. She determined in her heart to be God's woman. She wasted no time in wondering or worrying about what people thought of her—although she did care. She was as human as you and I, and she wanted to be liked and approved as we do—but, it was not uppermost in her mind. Ever!

My grandmother lived into her eighties. She was God's woman too, even though she was in great pain with arthritis and had been totally deaf for sixty of those years. She, too, cared what other people thought (especially other Hungarian women from her church), yet like my mother, human opinions were *always* secondary to God's opinion. He was their top priority.

When my brother, Cliff, was a marine corpsman in Vietnam, our mother was here in California, dying. Yet one of her last letters to him said, "Cliff, the Lord whispered so sweetly to me that if I put Him first—He'll see that I come in second." She wrote that, and it wasn't yet winter—only the autumn season. She never saw the winter.

My mother simply lived and died doing her best to impress the Lord. People mattered, but not more than the Lord. She had, indeed, fulfilled her commitment to the Lord by putting Him first—and, in my eyes, coming in second to God is not too shabby.

My mother also pointed me in the direction of Galatians 6. She knew the dangers of comparing ourselves to others, and as I grew older, she wanted to set some standards for growing in my heart and mind. She did this best through Scriptures.

Saint Paul wrote, "Let everyone be sure that he is doing his very best, for then he will have the personal satisfaction of work well done, and won't need to compare himself with someone else. Each of us must bear some faults and burdens of his own. For none of us is perfect" (Galatians 6:4,5 TLB).

This godly woman taught me that if God had gone to such great lengths to make each of us so magnificently original, it would be tacky of us to compare ourselves, feel jealousy, or be intimidated by someone else. "Do your best, honey, with what you've got, and leave the rest up to the Lord!" She meant those words—not only for the productive years of my life, but for the total sum as well. I was to do my best for the Lord right up until the moment He calls me home . . . and there had better be no slip-ups. I knew what my feelings and attitudes must be on aging.

Then, as if the Galatians verses were not enough, when I read The Living Bible's paraphrase of Proverbs 31, it was as if, for a brief moment, my mother's finger came out of heaven and carefully pointed out the verse.

"She has no fear of winter for her household, for she has made warm clothes for all of them" (Proverbs 31:21 TLB).

I could almost hear Mother whisper, "The Lord isn't only talking of clothing, but warm spiritual clothing as well. Teach your children in the ways of the Lord, so they will survive the winters of their lives."

I read on, and when I got to the twenty-fifth verse— "She is a woman of strength and dignity, and has no fear of old age"—I wept, because I knew I had just read a true description of my mother.

Both my mother and grandmother taught me by the consistent living of their lives. They particularly showed me how to joyously anticipate winter and how to dress warmly for the unavoidable storms of growing old.

Here are some of their distinctive, yet practical, lessons about this—the last of our changepoints. These precepts are just a part of the rich inheritance left to me, but I pray you will catch a glimpse of what God can do with your winter season.

Have a Well-Stocked Pantry of Praise

The descriptive phrases, "mean ole lady" and "crotchety old man," are not meaningless figments of some writer's imagination. They can be extremely accurate, unfortunately.

When we grow old, our bodies wear out and our bones grow brittle. But, more serious even than that, is the fact that we share the common fears of possible senility, and the loss of friends, interests, skills, and sexual abilities. These physical and mental conditions don't give rise to a rash of enthusiastic speeches by the elderly. In fact, many people facing the changepoint of old age are plagued by feelings of isolation and despair, and the natural result is a stream of nagging complaints, hostile comments, and even verbal abuse.

We all know that most of us will experience a fading of physical stamina and a decreasing capacity of our sensory skills. We won't see as well, hear as well, or remember things the way we used to, and that brings fear. Yet, the woman in Proverbs 31 was described as having "no fear of growing old." Remarkable.

Her secret was probably the ability to replace complaining with praising. Even if she had lived many more years, I'm sure she would have continued her life of positive praying and praising.

In everything (even growing old) we are told to give thanks. Our pantry shelves must be well stocked with jars of gratitude, appreciation for others, faith, and hope. Otherwise, we will starve to death during the winter of our lives.

My sister, Marilyn, who is twenty-nine and not a "complaining old woman," wrote about her own pantry shelves in her letter that read:

I heard a neat thought on complaining that has helped me not to complain as much—"People who have every reason to complain—*and don't,* are like Jesus!" That was special for me.

Every day I want to be able to say, "Lord, make me more like Jesus." And that hits in areas like complaining and hospitality. (Those are the two areas God has been personally dealing with me lately. I wish I could share all the hard growing pains the Lord has allowed me to go through concerning hospitality—wow—but it's been worth it!!!)

Well, to sum up in a nutshell what I am spiritually striving to do, is make this following prayer a part of my life. "Lord Jesus, if you were me, what would you be thinking, feeling and doing in this situation?" Boy, Joyce, I just about preached you a sermon, didn't I?

Marilyn is still in the spring and summer time of her life, yet she is preserving the right amounts of praise and thanksgiving for herself and her family's winter.

My grandmother's hands were terribly crippled by arthritis. She would tell me they hurt—when I asked. However, almost to the year of her death, she kept a spotless house, took meticulous care of her yard *and* garden, and walked to the neighborhood store for her own groceries nearly every day. She never became a mean ole lady, even though she was widowed, deaf, and crippled with painful arthritis. She replaced criticism and complaints with thankful praise.

Here are some WON'TS and WILLS I learned from my mother and grandmother for my winter siege.

I Won't	*I Will*
Bore everybody about my pain.	Accept my wrinkles for what they are: God-given experiences.
Give my children commandments.	Give my children suggestions.
Make my children feel guilty for not visiting or writing more often.	Gladly welcome visits from my grandchildren.
Talk about what foods disagree with me.	Try to eat less and exercise more.
Let my hair or personal grooming deteriorate.	Continue to ride my bicycle and swim.
Be impatient with my hard-of-hearing mate.	Keep on reading *everything*.
Pick or bicker with my mate over little stuff.	Keep a ready smile and a quick laugh always close to the surface.

Most importantly, never let your worries about the future keep you from seeing the changepoints of today. Of course, we must prepare for the future. It would be pure foolishness to be caught with our pantry shelves empty in the wintertime of our lives.

But it's also important to have a sane perspective about today—not some worried-to-death attitude that will cripple us and keep us from continuing to grow and bloom.

Put your yesterdays where they belong—in the past. Release yourself from time's mortgaging grip. The trouble, pain, and sorrow of yesterday is over. It's too late to change it.

God will forgive all your yesterdays if you trust in Christ. Rejoice with the Psalmist when he says, "What happiness for those whose guilt has been forgiven! What joys when sins are covered over! What relief for those who have confessed their sins and God has cleared their record."

There it is—the pantry shelves stocked with
   happiness,
      joy, and
         relief.

So, live today enthusiastically. It will expand your powers of appreciation. Perhaps you need to count your blessings each morning, then repeat, "This is the day which the Lord hath made; we will rejoice and be glad in it" (Psalms 118:24 KJV).

Welcome tomorrow with no nagging doubts as to its outcome. Remember, one morning the clouds will break open and Jesus will come back and we will be forever with Him!

Stoking the Memories' Fires

To ward off the chill of winter in our souls, we are going to have to bank and stoke the fires of our memories with many cords of experiences. None makes the heart warmer or the glow deeper than being God's woman as a grandmother.

I firmly believe every child should have at least one adult—not necessarily a "blood grandma"—but, one adult, who does *not* ask the child, "Have you brushed your teeth?" or "Have you combed your hair, straightened up your room, or fed the cat?" Every child deserves one adult like this. One adult who is not there to judge, supervise, instruct on weighty matters, but just to *enjoy* the child and their time together.

Dear women, especially those of you in the winter of your lives, find a child, *any child,* and be a grandma!

The program that is nearest and dearest to the heart of Nancy Reagan, our First Lady, is one which is sort of a lend-lease program for grandmothers and grandfathers. It pairs children with grandmas or grandpas; and both the adult and the child benefit from it. Both parties derive a great personal satisfaction from the shared friendship.

At this writing, I have three grandbabies, and they are the purest of joys to me.

Please don't ever say, "The best thing about having grandbabies is that when they have wet diapers or get sick you can give them back to their mothers"—for I'll probably rise up and punch your lights out. (Not really! But you get the picture?)

I'm rather allergic to that kind of a statement or philosophy, because I remember my own mother coming to visit me when both of my children were under three years of age.

She'd come in, pick up the first baby she came to, and say, "Oh, my. Your diapers are dirty. Let's get them changed." And off she'd go. From the living room I'd hear bits and pieces of dialogue, which sounded like this:

"Let's get you up here so Grandma can see you . . . oh, you're so darling . . . now, the pins . . . oh, dear, I forgot this stuff smelled so bad . . . Okay. Now, washie, washie . . . Mmmm . . . Smack, smack . . . (quick kisses) . . . I love you, Jesus loves you, and you're going to be a wonderful person . . . now, let's sprinkle the 'powpee' on . . . nice? Oh, you like powder . . . all set, now . . . I'm going to kiss your little gizzard . . . There, finished. Let's go back to the living room."

What transpired during those brief moments was *love* —spelled with a capital *L!* Besides, I—as Rick and Laurie's mother—had just changed thirty thousand diapers, and now *Grandma* was doing it. I'll never know who enjoyed it more, or who benefited from it the most, but I'm grateful that their grandmother didn't "give them back to their mother" with every dirty diaper or every high fever!

Do you remember, at the beginning of this book, I wrote that psychologists feel six-month-old babies know whether they are rejected or loved by the way they are handled and diapered? Well, it's really true. And this is your chance, and mine, to really program love into those babies' little computers and give it all we've got.

Maybe you're suffering from guilt because you feel you failed your children. Perhaps you weren't a Christian. Maybe you were ill. But, in any case, you're not too happy about the standards of motherhood you kept. Here's some cheering news. Now, as a grandmother, you have another chance, a new start, and a fresh opportunity to be the woman God wants you to be. Use all those hard-learned lessons to their best advantage and be the greatest grandma in the world.

Even *busy* grandmothers still have more time than mothers to listen, to enjoy, and to encourage these precious little ones.

I'm barely inside the door of Rick and Teresa's house when my four-year-old granddaughter, April Joy, says, "Grandma Joyce, I have some things I'd like to talk to you about. Can we go into my room and talk?"

I say yes, and off we go. I sit on the floor, she stands beside me so we can look eyeball-to-eyeball, and then she starts in . . . preschool, friends, toys, anything . . . but it's all about her little world.

Once, while we were chatting, her dad opened the door to call us for dinner. She looked over at him and said sweetly, "Please close the door, Dad, we aren't finished yet."

I hope we never finish. I want to influence April, Richard, and James with my love. I want to bring Jesus to them in the only way I know how—by loving them into His care and keeping.

Surely, there is a child near you whom you can invest in and thereby stoke your memories' fire for the winter ahead.

Looking Forward to Spring

Of all the multitude of tragedies in growing old, the forfeiting of a dream, the losing of hope, and the failure to look forward to spring are the greatest.

You and I, no matter what age we are, have some choices and alternatives. Did you know that? Well, we do! We can't predict whether this year will be good or bad; if it will bring sickness or health; if it will be economically up or down; or, even if this winter will be our last. But, we do have some choices.

We can keep our dreams and hopes alive, or we can kill them. We can dwell in the past, pine away for the future, or live today . . . here and now.

Dreams, hopes, and looking forward were very much alive in the lives of the people listed below:

Grandma Moses was almost eighty when she *started* to paint.

Blind Fanny Crosby was almost sixty when she wrote the first of hundreds of our choice hymns.

Thomas Edison was labeled "too stupid to learn," yet he was one of the greatest inventors of his time—right up until he died.

Bill Wilson was once a "hopeless" alcoholic, yet he was the founder of Alcoholics Anonymous.

John Milton was blinded at age forty-four. Sixteen years later, he wrote "Paradise Lost."

Winston Churchill flunked the sixth grade and was considered a dull and hopeless student. Yet, in the autumn and the winter of his life, he led England to victory in World War II.

James E. West was a crippled child whose only home was an orphanage. Yet, he became the first chief executive of the Boy Scouts of America.

Ronald Reagan, at the age of sixty-nine, became the fortieth President of the United States.

Corrie ten Boom was in her early fifties when she was released from Ravensbruck concentration camp, after she had lost her entire family. Four decades later, she has continued to introduce untold thousands of people to her friend, Jesus.

(Incidentally, Joyce Landorf was thirty-seven when, with no training or journalistic education at all, she was asked to write books. She has written fourteen in twelve years.)

I could go on, but the message here, I think, is clear. Don't bury your dreams or your hopes. Keep them out and alive. Keep looking forward to spring.

The Apostle Paul was sick and dying when he wrote to his spiritual adopted son, Timothy, "My time has almost run out. Very soon now I will be on my way to heaven. I have fought long and hard for my Lord, and through it all I have kept true to him. And now the time has come for me to stop fighting and rest. In heaven a crown is waiting for me which the Lord, the righteous Judge, will give me on that great day of his return . . ." (2 Timothy 4:6–8 TLB).

Here it is, Paul is dying, after serving the Lord some thirty-five years, yet he does not merely lie down and wait for death's appointment. A few verses later, he asks Timothy to do four things . . .

1. "Please come as soon as you can . . . and bring Mark with you. . . ." Luke was already there, but Paul knew the immense value of having friends with him in his old age.

2. "When you come, be sure to bring the coat I left. . . ." Paul, although old and sick, was going to take care of his physical body, his temple of the Holy Spirit, to the best of his ability. Many times, the older people grow, the less they take care of their bodies; and Paul, knowing that, asked for his coat so he could ward off any sickness that could come with the dampness.

3. "Be sure to bring . . . the books. . . ." Paul was still in the process of learning and stretching his mind. He kept up his reading, even though he was dying.

4. "Be sure to bring . . . the books, but especially the parchments." Paul wanted the Scriptures to be right there with him, so his soul could continue to prosper.

Blessed, dying Paul ends his letter to Timothy with these succinct words, "Do try to be here before winter."

Paul was a man who never stopped looking forward. Even in the last moments of his life, he kept his dreams and hopes alive.

Before I put down my pen, let me leave you with one more observation:

I don't know which changepoint of life you're in, I don't know how you're faring, but I do know it's the changepoint when you need the Lord the most. Why? Because it's the *now* place of your life.

Not long ago, April Joy was visiting us. It was Saturday night, and I wanted to prepare her for church the next morning.

"Guess what, April?"

"What, Grandma Joyce?"

"Tomorrow is Sunday! You're going to wear your new shoes, your Sunday dress, and we are all going to church!"

I want her to love going to church. I don't want to drag her there, or sit on her after she gets there. I want to make it so exciting she can't stand *not* to be there. So, I really revved up her little motor about how wonderful it would be tomorrow, to go to church.

Then, I realized that my husband, Dick, was chairman of the finance committee, and tomorrow he'd have to sit on the platform to give a report. I play the piano for the congregation and choir, so I would be at the piano. And April would have to sit alone in the front row. I thought, quickly, I'd better prepare her for the worst.

"There's just one thing, honey," I explained. "Papa has to sit on the platform beside Pastor Jim, and I have to be at the piano. I won't be able to sit with you until the sermon."

April thought about that for one split second and then answered brightly, "Okay. Then, I'll sing and dance!" (Dance?)

No hesitation, no doubts, and no sad face. There was a choice to be made, and April made it with the most enthusiastic spirit I've ever seen. Her contribution to the service would be singing and dancing—opposed to crying or pouting. Good girl!

Do you know that every night of your life, God gives you the same opportunity of choice? He really does. Whatever changepoint you are in, no matter who you are, how old you are, who you are married to, or if you are alone, God gives you a tomorrow.

He whispers down to you each night, "Guess what . . . tomorrow is a new day, and I'm giving it to you." Then

He gently prepares you. He tells you that tomorrow might hold some sorrow, some hurts, some loneliness—and, Satan or even an enemy may try their best to destroy you —but that *He knows what He is doing.*

What is your response? You have a choice. You can accept His gift, or you can turn away from it. You may respond with, "Oh, Lord, I can't bear tomorrow. I don't want it, and I'm not going to put on my clothes and go through with tomorrow."Or, you can say, as April did, "Okay! Then I'll sing and dance! I'll do it, Lord! I'll take tomorrow as my gift from you! I'll listen closely to Your music. And I'll do my very best! I'll do it because I trust You, Jesus, and because I believe You know what You're doing!"

For just this quiet moment, put this book down and sing Kurt Kaiser's beautiful song with me.

> Oh how He loves you and me.
> Oh how He loves you and me.
> He gave His life—what more could He give?
> Oh how He loves me,
> Oh how He loves you—
> Oh how He loves you and me.

He does, you know, and He will continue to love you throughout every changepoint of your life!

Just think, there will come a day, a brilliant, gorgeous day, when all our changepoints will be behind us. We'll see Jesus face-to-face, and we will be forever and ever changed into His likeness, to never change again. Hold that thought!

Even so, Lord Jesus, come quickly!

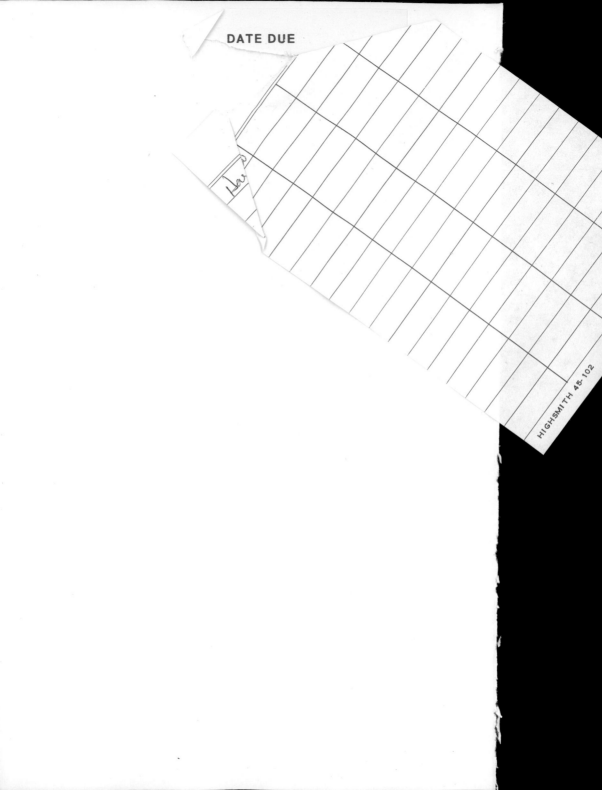